PSB Health Occupations Aptitude Exam Study Guide

Test Prep Secrets for the PSB HOAE

Printed in the United States of America

Table of Contents

Introduction

Congratulations on your decision to join the field of nursing - few other professions are so rewarding!

By purchasing this book, you've already made the first step towards succeeding in your career; and the second step is to do well on the PSB-HOAE. The Health Occupations Aptitude Examination (HOAE) will require you to demonstrate knowledge and competence of those subjects taught at the high school level.

This book will help refresh you on all of those subjects, as well as provide you with some inside-information on how to do well on this test. Even if it's been years since you've graduated high school, studied, or taken a test – don't worry, you'll be ready!

About the Test

The PSB-HOAE is administered by the Psychological Services Bureau; it consists of 360 questions, divided into the following subjects:

1. **Academic Aptitude**
    - Arithmetic
        - 30 Questions: Math at the Eighth-Grade Level.
    - Vocabulary
        - 30 Questions: Knowledge of Vocabulary.
    - Non-Verbal
        - 30 Questions: Comprehension of Spatial Relationships.
2. **Spelling**
    - 50 Questions: Spelling and Word Knowledge.
3. **Reading**
    - 40 Questions: Reading Comprehension.
4. **Natural Sciences**
    - 90 Questions: Knowledge of Elementary-Level Biology, Chemistry, & Health.
5. **Vocational Adjustment Index**
    - 90 Questions: Evaluates Your Attitude, Feelings, and Characteristic/Behavioral Traits.

Scoring

You cannot "pass" or "fail" the PSB-HOAE. Your score is simply indicative of your current level of comprehension. However, each school has their own entrance requirements – some are higher than others. Be sure to check with the requirements of the institutions which you want to attend.

You will, however, be given a percentile score. This is not an indication of how many questions you answered correctly on the exam – rather, it shows how well you did in comparison to other test-takers.

How This Book Works

The subsequent chapters in this book are divided into a review of those topics covered on the exam. This is not intended to "teach" or "re-teach" you these concepts – there is no way to cram all of that material into one book! Instead, we are going to help you recall all of the information which you've already learned. Even more importantly, we'll show you how to apply that knowledge.

Each chapter includes an extensive review, with practice drills at the end to test your knowledge. With time, practice, and determination, you'll be well-prepared for test day.

Chapter 1: Arithmetic

The math section of the PSB-HOAE consists of basic algebra, geometry, and applied math. All core concepts you need to know for the exam will be covered in detail in this chapter.

The Most Common Mistakes

People make mistakes all the time – but during a test, those mistakes can make the difference between an excellent score, or one which falls below the requirements. Watch out for these common mistakes that people make on the HOAE:

- Answering with the wrong sign (positive / negative).
- Mixing up the Order of Operations.
- Misplacing a decimal.
- Not reading the question thoroughly (and therefore providing an answer that was not asked for.)
- Circling the wrong letter, or filling in wrong circle choice.

If you're thinking, "Those ideas are just common sense" – exactly! Most of the mistakes made on the HOAE are simple mistakes. Regardless, they still result in a wrong answer and the loss of a potential point.

Strategies for the Arithmetic Section

1. **Go Back to the Basics**: First and foremost, practice your basic skills: sign changes, order of operations, simplifying fractions, and equation manipulation. These are the skills used most on the HOAE, though they are applied in different contexts. Remember that when it comes right down to it, all math problems rely on the four basic skills of addition, subtraction, multiplication, and division. All that changes is the order in which they are used to solve a problem.

2. **Don't Rely on Mental Math**: Using mental math is great for eliminating answer choices, but ALWAYS WRITE IT DOWN! This cannot be stressed enough. Use whatever paper is provided; by writing and/or drawing out the problem, you are more likely to catch any mistakes. The act of writing things down forces you to organize your calculations, leading to an improvement in your HOAE score. Use your calculator to *check* your work.

3. **The Three-Times Rule**:

    - **Step One – Read the question**: Write out the given information.
    - **Step Two – Read the question**: Set up your equation(s) and solve.
    - **Step Three – Read the question:** Make sure that your answer makes sense (is the amount too large or small, is the answer in the correct unit of measure, etc.).

4. **Make an Educated Guess**: Eliminate those answer choices which you are relatively sure are incorrect, and then guess from the remaining choices. Educated guessing is critical to increasing your score.

Math Concepts Tested on the HOAE

You need to practice in order to score well on the test. To make the most out of your practice, use this guide to determine the areas for which you need more review. Most importantly, practice all areas under testing circumstances (a quiet area, a timed practice test, no looking up facts as you practice, etc.)

When reviewing, take your time and let your brain recall the necessary math. If you are taking the HOAE, then you have already had course instruction in these areas. The examples given will "jog" your memory.

The next few pages will cover various math subjects (starting with the basics, but in no particular order), along with worked examples.

Order of Operations

PEMDAS – **P**arentheses/**E**xponents/**M**ultiply/**D**ivide/**A**dd/**S**ubtract

Perform the operations within parentheses first, and then any exponents. After those steps, perform all multiplication and division. (These are done from left to right, as they appear in the problem) Finally, do all required addition and subtraction, also from left to right as they appear in the problem.

Examples:

Solve $(-(2)^2 - (4 + 7))$

$(-4 - 11) = \mathbf{-15}$

Solve $((5)^2 \div 5 + 4 * 2)$

$25 \div 5 + 4 * 2$

$5 + 8 = \mathbf{13}$

Positive & Negative Number Rules

(+) + (-) = Subtract the two numbers. Solution gets the sign of the larger number.

(-) + (-) = Negative number.

(-) * (-) = Positive number.

(-) * (+) = Negative number.

(-) / (-) = Positive number.

(-) / (+) = Negative number.

Fractions

Adding and subtracting fractions requires a common denominator.

Find a common denominator for:

$$\frac{2}{3} - \frac{1}{5}$$

$$\frac{2}{3} - \frac{1}{5} = \frac{2}{3}\left(\frac{5}{5}\right) - \frac{1}{5}\left(\frac{3}{3}\right) = \frac{10}{15} - \frac{3}{15} = \mathbf{\frac{7}{15}}$$

To add mixed fractions, work first the whole numbers, and then the fractions.

$$2\frac{1}{4} + 1\frac{3}{4} = 3\frac{4}{4} = \mathbf{4}$$

To subtract mixed fractions, convert to single fractions by multiplying the whole number by the denominator and adding the numerator. Then work as above.

$$2\frac{1}{4} - 1\frac{3}{4} = \frac{9}{4} - \frac{7}{4} = \frac{2}{4} = \mathbf{\frac{1}{2}}$$

To multiply fractions, convert any mixed fractions into single fractions and multiply across; reduce to lowest terms if needed.

$$2\frac{1}{4} * 1\frac{3}{4} = \frac{9}{4} * \frac{7}{4} = \frac{63}{16} = \mathbf{3\frac{15}{16}}$$

To divide fractions, convert any mixed fractions into single fractions, flip the second fraction, and then multiply across.

$$2\frac{1}{4} \div 1\frac{3}{4} = \frac{9}{4} \div \frac{7}{4} = \frac{9}{4} * \frac{4}{7} = \frac{36}{28} = 1\frac{8}{28} = \mathbf{1\frac{2}{7}}$$

Absolute Value

The absolute value of a number is its distance from zero, not its value.

So in $|x| = a$, "x" will equal "$-a$" as well as "a."

Likewise, $| 3 | = 3$, and $| -3 | = 3$.

Equations with absolute values will have two answers. Solve each absolute value possibility separately. All solutions must be checked into the original equation.

Example: Solve for x:

$|2x - 3| = x + 1$

Equation One: $2x - 3 = -(x + 1)$

$2x - 3 = -x - 1$

$3x = 2$

$\mathbf{x = 2/3}$

Equation Two: $2x - 3 = x + 1$

$\mathbf{x = 4}$

Greatest Common Factor (GCF)

The greatest factor that divides two numbers.

Example: The GCF of 24 and 18 is 6. 6 is the largest number, or greatest factor, that can divide both 24 and 18.

Mean, Median, Mode

Mean is a math term for "average." Total all terms and divide by the number of terms.

Find the mean of 24, 27, and 18.

24 + 27 + 18 = 69 ÷ 3 = **23**

Median is the middle number of a given set, found after the numbers have all been put in numerical order. In the case of a set of even numbers, the middle two numbers are averaged.

What is the median of 24, 27, and 18?

18, **24**, 27

What is the median of 24, 27, 18, and 19?

18, 19, 24, 27 (19 + 24 = 43. 43/2 = **21.5**)

Mode is the number which occurs most frequently within a given set.

What is the mode of 2, 5, 4, 4, 3, 2, 8, 9, 2, 7, 2, and 2?

The mode would be **2** because it appears the most within the set.

Percent, Part, & Whole

Part = Percent * Whole

Percent = Part / Whole

Whole = Part / Percent

Example: Jim spent 30% of his paycheck at the fair. He spent $15 for a hat, $30 for a shirt, and $20 playing games. How much was his check? (Round to nearest dollar)

Whole = 65 / .30 = $**217.00**

Percent Change

Percent Change = amount of change / original amount * 100

Percent Increase =
(new amount – original amount) / original amount * 100

Percent Decrease =
(original amount – new amount) / original amount * 100

Amount Increase (or Decrease) =
original price * percent markup (or markdown)

Original price = new price / (whole - percent markdown)

Original price = new price / (whole + percent markup)

Example: A car that was originally priced at $8300 has been reduced to $6995. What percent has it been reduced?

(8300 – 6995) / 8300 * 100 = **15.72%**

Repeated Percent Change

Increase: Final amount = original amount * $(1 + \text{rate})^{\#\text{ of changes}}$

Decrease: Final Amount = original amount * $(1 - \text{rate})^{\#\text{ of changes}}$

Example: The weight of a tube of toothpaste decreases by 3% each time it is used. If it weighed 76.5 grams when new, what is its weight in grams after 15 uses?

Final amount = $76.5 * (1 - .3)^{15}$
$76.5 * (.97)^{15}$ = **48.44 grams**

Simple Interest

Interest * Principle

Example: If I deposit $500 into an account with an annual rate of 5%, how much will I have after 2 years?

1st year: 500 + (500*.05) = 525

2nd year: 525 + (525*.05) = **551.25**

Ratios

To solve a ratio, simply find the equivalent fraction. To distribute a whole across a ratio:

1. Total all parts.
2. Divide the whole by the total number of parts.
3. Multiply quotient by corresponding part of ratio.

Example: There are 90 voters in a room, and they are either Democrat or Republican. The ratio of Democrats to Republicans is 5:4. How many Republicans are there?

Step 1 5 + 4 = 9

Step 2 90 / 9 = 10

Step 3 10 * 4 = **40 Republicans**

Proportions

Direct Proportions: Corresponding ratio parts change in the same direction (increase/decrease).

Indirect Proportions: Corresponding ratio parts change in opposite directions (as one part increases the other decreases).

Example: A train traveling 120 miles takes 3 hours to get to its destination. How long will it take if the train travels 180 miles?

120 mph:180 mph is to x hours:3 hours.
(Write as fraction and cross multiply.)

$120/3 = 180/x$

$540 = 120x$

x = **4.5 hours**

Probabilities

A probability is found by dividing the number of desired outcomes by the number of possible outcomes. (The piece divided by the whole.)

Example: What is the probability of picking a blue marble if 3 of the 15 marbles are blue?

3/15 = 1/5. The probability is **1 in 5** that a blue marble is picked

Arithmetic Sequence

Each term is equal to the previous term plus x.

Example: 2, 5, 8, 11

$\mathbf{x = 3}$

$2 + 3 = 5$; $5 + 3 = 8$ … etc.

Geometric Sequence

Each term is equal to the previous term multiplied by x.

Example: 2, 4, 8, 16

$\mathbf{x = 2}$

Prime Factorization

Expand to prime number factors.

Example: 104 = 2 * 2 * 2 * 13

Exponent Rules

Rule	Example
$x^0 = 1$	$5^0 = 1$
$x^1 = x$	$5^1 = 5$
$x^a \cdot x^b = x^{a+b}$	$5^2 * 5^3 = 5^5$
$(xy)^a = x^a y^a$	$(5 * 6)^2 = 5^2 * 6^2 = 25 * 36$
$(x^a)^b = x^{ab}$	$(5^2)^3 = 5^6$
$(x/y)^a = x^a/y^a$	$(10/5)^2 = 10^2/5^2 = 100/25$
$x^a/y^b = x^{a-b}$	$5^4/5^3 = 5^1 = 5$ (remember $x \neq 0$)
$x^{1/a} = \sqrt[a]{x}$	$25^{1/2} = \sqrt[2]{25} = 5$
$x^{-a} = \frac{1}{x^a}$	$5^{-2} = \frac{1}{5^2} = \frac{1}{25}$ (remember $x \neq 0$)
$(-x)^a$ = positive number if "a" is even; negative number if "a" is odd.	

Roots

Root of a Product: $\sqrt[n]{a \cdot b} = \sqrt[n]{a} \cdot \sqrt[n]{b}$

Root of a Quotient: $\sqrt[n]{\frac{a}{b}} = \frac{\sqrt[n]{a}}{\sqrt[n]{b}}$

Fractional Exponent: $\sqrt[n]{a^{m}} = a^{m/n}$

Literal Equations

Equations with more than one variable. Solve in terms of one variable first.

Example: Solve for y: $4x + 3y = 3x + 2y$

Step 1 – Combine like terms: $3y - 2y = 4x - 2x$

Step 2 – Solve for y: $\mathbf{y = 2x}$

Slope

The formula used to calculate the slope (m) of a straight line connecting two points is: $m = (y_2 - y_1) / (x_2 - x_1)$ = change in y / change in x.

Example:

Calculate slope of the line in the diagram:

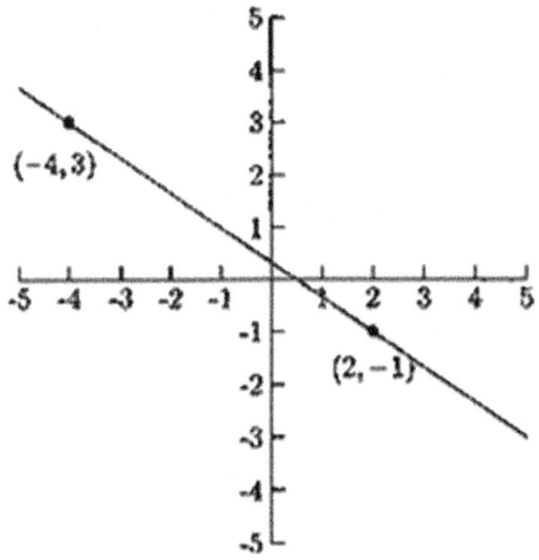

$m = (3 - (-1))/(-4 - 2) = 4/-6 =$ **- 2/3**

Midpoint

To determine the midpoint between two points, simply add the two x coordinates together and divide by 2 (midpoint x). Then add the y coordinates together and divide by 2 (midpoint y).

$$\left(\frac{x_1 + x_2}{2}, \frac{y_1 + y}{2}\right)$$

Algebraic Equations

When simplifying or solving algebraic equations, you need to be able to utilize all math rules: exponents, roots, negatives, order of operations, etc.

1. Add & Subtract: Only the coefficients of like terms.

   Example:

   $5xy + 7y + 2yz + 11xy - 5yz = 16xy + 7y - 3yz$

2. Multiplication: First the coefficients then the variables.

   Example: monomial * monomial

   $(3x^4y^2z)(2y^4z^5) = 6x^4y^6z^6$

   (A variable with no exponent has an implied exponent of 1)

   Example: monomial * polynomial

   $(2y^2)(y^3+2xy^2z + 4z) = 2y^5 + 4xy^4z + 8y^2z$

   Example: binomial * binomial

   $(5x + 2)(3x + 3)$

   (Remember FOIL – First, Outer, Inner, Last)

   First: $5x * 3x = 15x^2$

   Outer: $5x * 3 = 15x$

   Inner: $2 * 3x = 6x$

   Last: $2 * 3 = 6$

   Combine like terms: $15x^2 + 21x + 6$

   Example: binomial * polynomial

   $(x + 3)(2x^2 - 5x - 2)$

   First term: $x(2x^2 - 5x - 2) = 2x^3 - 5x^2 - 2x$

   Second term: $3(2x^2 - 5x - 2) = 6x^2 - 15x - 6$

   Added Together: $2x^3 + x^2 - 17x - 6$

Inequalities

Inequalities are solved like linear and algebraic equations, except the sign must be reversed when dividing by a negative number.

Example: $-7x + 2 < 6 - 5x$

Step 1 – Combine like terms: $-2x < 4$

Step 2 – Solve for x. (Reverse the sign): $\boldsymbol{x > -2}$

Solving compound inequalities will give you two answers.

Example: $-4 \leq 2x - 2 \leq 6$

Step 1 – Add 2 to each term to isolate x: $-2 \leq 2x \leq 8$

Step 2: Divide by 2: $-1 \leq x \leq 4$

Solution set is **[-1, 4]**

Fundamental Counting Principle

(The number of possibilities of an event happening) * (the number of possibilities of another event happening) = the total number of possibilities.

Example:

If you take a multiple choice test with 5 questions, with 4 answer choices for each question, how many test result possibilities are there?

Solution:

Question 1 has 4 choices; question 2 has 4 choices; etc.

4 *4 * 4 * 4 * 4 (one for each question) = **1024 possible test results.**

Permutations

The number of ways a set number of items can be arranged. Recognized by the use of a factorial (n!), with n being the number of items.

If n = 3, then 3! = 3 * 2 * 1 = 6. If you need to arrange n number of things but *x* number are alike, then n! is divided by *x*!

Example:

How many different ways can the letters in the word **balance** be arranged?

Solution:

There are 7 letters so *n! =* 7*!* and 2 letters are the same so *x! =* 2*!* Set up the equation:

$$\frac{7* 6* 5* 4* 3* 2* 1}{2* 1} = \textbf{2540 ways.}$$

Combinations

To calculate total number of possible combinations use the formula:
n!/r! (n-r)!   n = # of objects   r = # of objects selected at a time

Example:

If seven people are selected in groups of three, how many different combinations are possible?

Solution:

$$\frac{7* 6* 5* 4* 3* 2* 1}{(3*2* 1)(7-3)} = \textbf{210 possible combinations.}$$

Geometry

- **Acute Angle**: Measures less than 90°.
- **Acute Triangle**: Each angle measures less than 90°.
- **Obtuse Angle**: Measures greater than 90°.
- **Obtuse Triangle**: One angle measures greater than 90°.
- **Adjacent Angles**: Share a side and a vertex.
- **Complementary Angles**: Adjacent angles that sum to 90°.
- **Supplementary Angles**: Adjacent angles that sum to 180°.
- **Vertical Angles**: Angles that are opposite of each other. They are always congruent (equal in measure).
- **Equilateral Triangle**: All angles are equal.
- **Isosceles Triangle**: Two sides and two angles are equal.
- **Scalene**: No equal angles.
- **Parallel Lines**: Lines that will never intersect. Y **ll** X means line Y is parallel to line X.
- **Perpendicular lines**: Lines that intersect or cross to form 90° angles.
- **Transversal Line**: A line that crosses parallel lines.
- **Bisector**: Any line that cuts a line segment, angle, or polygon exactly in half.
- **Polygon**: Any enclosed plane shape with three or more connecting sides (ex. a triangle).
- **Regular Polygon**: Has all equal sides and equal angles (ex. square).
- **Arc**: A portion of a circle's edge.
- **Chord**: A line segment that connects two different points on a circle.
- **Tangent**: Something that touches a circle at only one point without crossing through it.
- **Sum of Angles**: The sum of angles of a polygon can be calculated using $(n-1)180^o$, when n = the number of sides

Know the Names of Sided Plane Figures:

Number of Sides	Name
11	Hendecagon
12	Dodecagon
13	Tridecagon
14	Tetradecagon
15	Pentadecagon
16	Hexadecagon
17	Heptadecagon
18	Octadecagon
10	Decagon

Number of Sides	Name
3	Triangle (or Trigon)
4	Quadrilateral (or Tetragon)
5	Pentagon
6	Hexagon
7	Heptagon
8	Octagon
9	Nonagon

Regular Polygons

Polygon Angle Principle: S = The sum of interior angles of a polygon with n-sides.

$$S = (n - 2)180$$

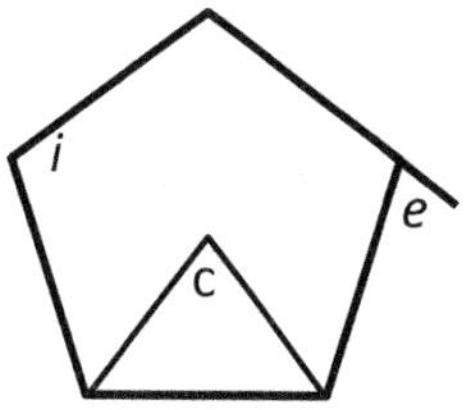

The measure of each central angle (c) is $360°/n$.

The measure of each interior angle (i) is $(n - 2)180°/n$.

The measure of each exterior angle (e) is $360°/n$.

To compare areas of similar polygons:

$$A_1/A_2 = (side_1/side_2)^2$$

Triangles

The angles in a triangle add up to 180°.

Area of a triangle = ½ * b * h, or ½bh.

Pythagoras' Theorem: $a^2 + b^2 = c^2$.

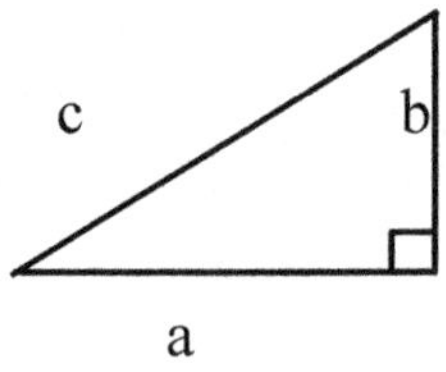

Trapezoids

Four-sided polygon, in which the bases (and only the bases) are parallel.

Isosceles Trapezoid – base angles are congruent.

Area and Perimeter of a Trapezoid

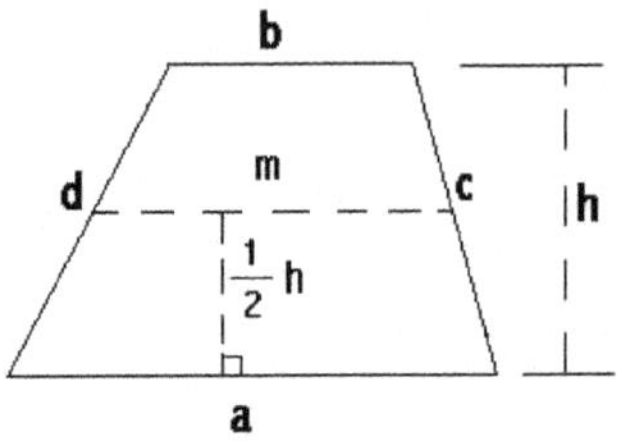

$$m = \frac{1}{2}(a + b)$$

$$Area = \frac{1}{2} h * (a + b) = m * h$$

$$Perimeter = a + b + c + d = 2m + c + d$$

If m is the median then: $m \parallel \overline{AB}$ and $m \parallel CD$

Rhombus

Four-sided polygon, in which all four sides are congruent and opposite sides are parallel.

Area and Perimeter of a Rhombus

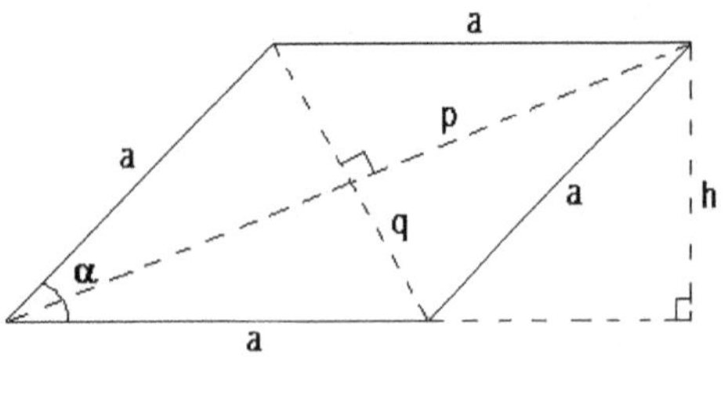

$$Perimeter = 4a$$

$$Area = a^2 \sin\alpha = a * h = \frac{1}{2}pq$$

$$4a^2 = p^2 + q^2$$

Rectangle

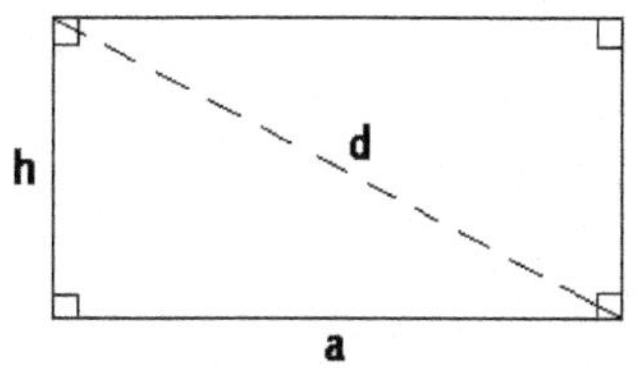

Area and Perimeter of a Rectangle

$d = \sqrt{a^2 + h^2}$

$a = \sqrt{d^2 - h^2}$

$h = \sqrt{d^2 - a^2}$

$Perimeter = 2a + 2h$

$Area = a \cdot h$

Square

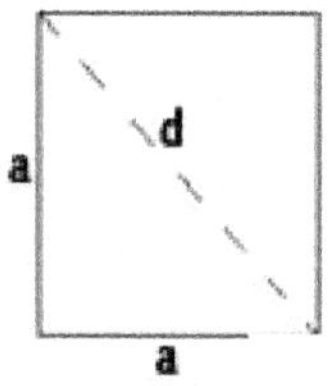

Area and Perimeter of a Square

$d = a\sqrt{2}$

$Perimeter = 4a = 2d\sqrt{2}$

$Area = a^2 = \frac{1}{2}d^2$

Circle

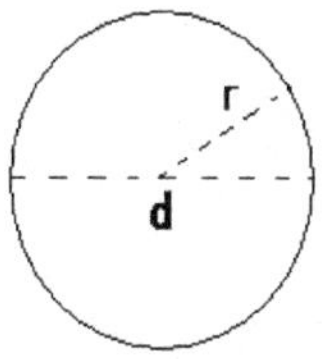

Area and Perimeter of a Circle

$d = 2r$

$Perimeter = 2\pi r = \pi d$

$Area = \pi r^2$

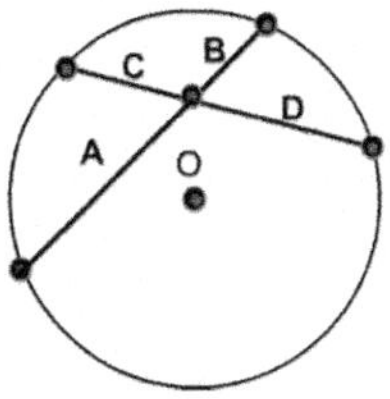

The product length of one chord equals the product length of the other, or:

AB=CD

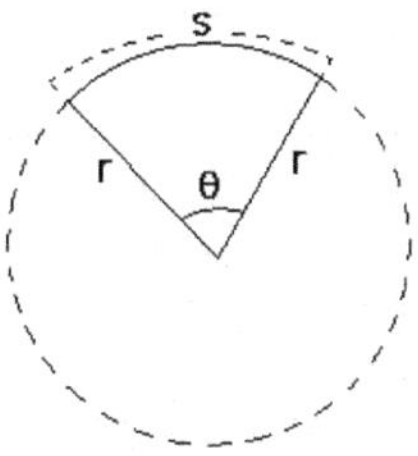

Area and Perimeter of the Sector of a Circle

$\alpha = \frac{\theta\pi}{180}\ (rad)$

$s = r\alpha$

$Perimeter = 2r + s$

$Area = \frac{1}{2}\theta\, r^2\ (radians)\ or\ \frac{n}{360}\pi r^2$

length (l) of an arc $l = \frac{\pi n r}{180}$ *or* $\frac{n}{360} 2\pi r$

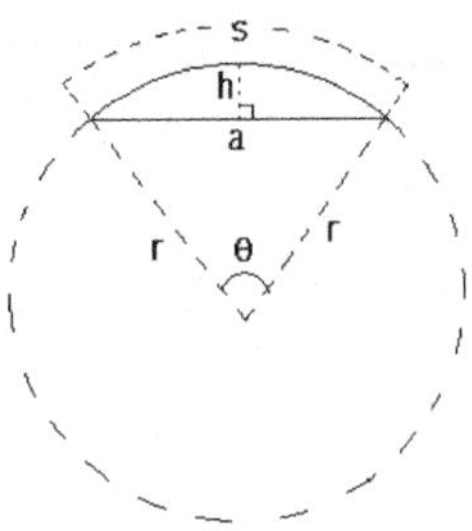

Area and Perimeter of the Segment of a Circle

$$\alpha = \frac{\theta\pi}{180}\ (rad)$$

$$a = 2\sqrt{2hr - h^2}$$

$$a^2 = 2r^2 - 2r^2\cos\theta$$

$$s = r\alpha$$

$$h = r - \frac{1}{2}\sqrt{4r^2 - a^2}$$

$$Perimeter = a + s$$

$$Area = \frac{1}{2}[sr - a(r - h)]$$

Cube

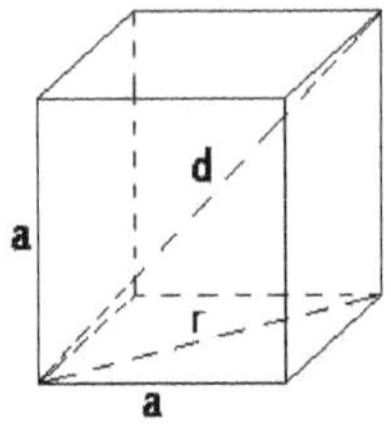

Area and Volume of a Cube

$$r = a\sqrt{2}$$

$$d = a\sqrt{3}$$

$$Area = 6a^2$$

$$Volume = a^3$$

Cuboid

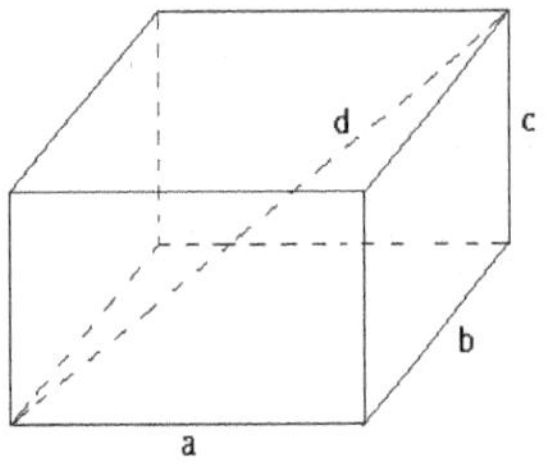

Area and Volume of a Cuboid

$$d = \sqrt{a^2 + b^2 + c^2}$$

$$A = 2(ab + ac + bc)$$

$$V = abc$$

Pyramid

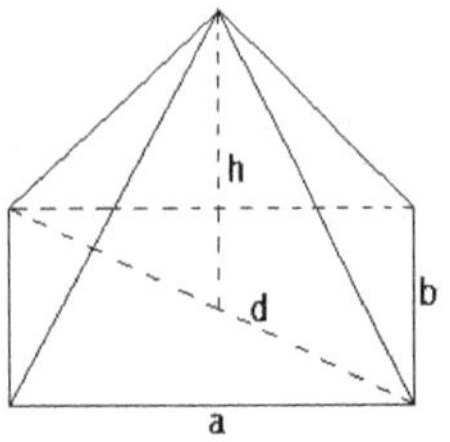

Area and Volume of a Pyramid

$$A_{lateral} = a\sqrt{h^2 + \left(\frac{b}{2}\right)^2} + b\sqrt{h^2 + \left(\frac{a}{2}\right)^2}$$

$$d = \sqrt{a^2 + b^2}$$

$$A_{base} = ab$$

$$A_{total} = A_{lateral} + A_{base}$$

$$V = \frac{1}{3}abh$$

Cylinder

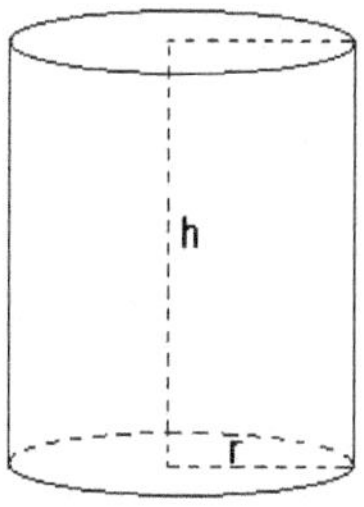

Area and Volume of a Cylinder

$d = 2r$

$A_{surface} = 2\pi r h$

$A_{base} = 2\pi r^2$

$Area = A_{surface} + A_{base}$

$= 2\pi r\,(h + r)$

$Volume = \pi r^2 h$

Cone

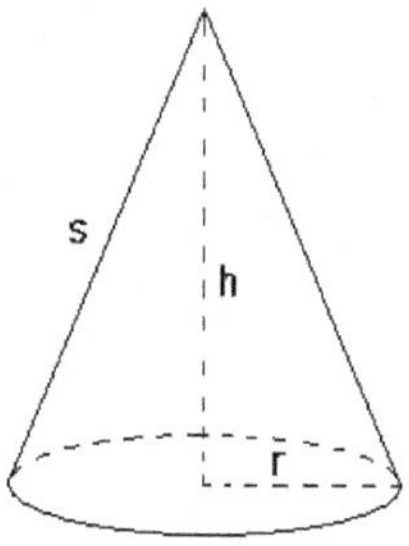

Area and Volume of a Cone

$d = 2r$

$A_{surface} = \pi r s$

$A_{base} = \pi r^2$

$Area = A_{surface} + A_{base}$

$= 2\pi r\,(h + r)$

$Volume = \frac{1}{3}\pi r^2 h$

Sphere

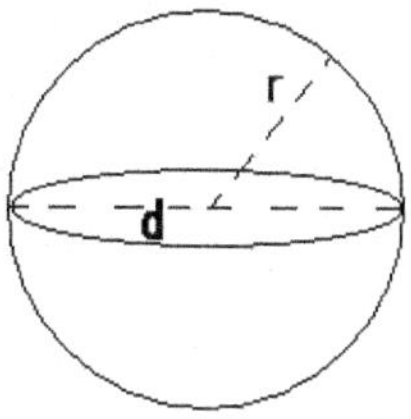

Area and Volume of a Sphere

$d = 2r$

$A_{surface} = 4\pi r^2$

$Volume = \frac{4}{3}\pi r^3$

Test Your Knowledge: Arithmetic Question Bank

Test Your Knowledge: Percent/Part/Whole, Percent Change

1. In a class of 42 students, 18 are boys. Two girls get transferred to another school. What percent of students remaining are girls?

a) 14%.
b) 16%.
c) 52.4%.
d) 60%.
e) None of the above.

2. A payroll check is issued for $500.00. If 20% goes to bills, 30% of the remainder goes to pay entertainment expenses, and 10% of what is left is placed in a retirement account, then approximately how much is remaining?

a) $150.
b) $250.
c) $170.
d) $350.
e) $180.

3. A painting by Van Gogh increased in value by 80% from year 1995 to year 2000. If in year 2000, the painting is worth $7200, what was its value in 1995?

a) $1500.
b) $2500.
c) $3000.
d) $4000.
e) $5000.

4. "Dresses and Ties" sells a particular dress for $60 dollars. But, they decide to discount the price of that dress by 25%. How much does the dress cost now?

a) $55.
b) $43.
c) $45.
d) $48.
e) $65.

5. A sweater goes on sale for 30% off. If the original price was $70, what is the discounted price?

a) $48.
b) $49.
c) $51.
d) $65.
e) $52.

6. If the value of a car depreciates by 60% over ten years, and its value in the year 2000 is $2500, what was its value in the year 1990?

a) $6000.
b) $6230.
c) $6250.
d) $6500.
e) $6600.

7. If an account is opened with a starting balance of \$500, what is the amount in the account after 3 years if the account pays compound interest of 5%?

a) \$560.80.
b) \$578.81.
c) \$564.50.
d) \$655.10.
e) \$660.00.

8. A piece of memorabilia depreciates by 1% every year. If the value of the memorabilia is \$75000, what will it be 2 years from now? Give the answer as a whole number.

a) \$74149.
b) \$74150.
c) \$73151.
d) \$71662.
e) \$73507.

9. A dress is marked down by 20% in an effort to boost sales for one week. After that week, the price of the dress is brought back to the original value. What percent did the price of the dress have to be increased from its discounted price?

a) 20%.
b) 25%.
c) 120%.
d) 125%.
e) 15%.

10. A car dealer increases the price of a car by 30%, but then discounts it by 30%. What is the relationship between the final price and the original price?

a) $.91x : x$.
b) $.98x : x$.
c) 1:1.
d) $.88x : x$.
e) $.75x : x$.

Test Your Knowledge: Percent/Part/Whole, Percent – Answers

1. **e)**
   The entire class has 42 students, 18 of which are boys, meaning 42 - 18 = 24 is the number of girls. Out of these 24 girls, 2 leave; so 22 girls are left. The total number of students is now 42 - 2 = 40.

   22/40 * 100 = 55%.

   Reminder: If you forget to subtract 2 from the total number of students, you will end up with 60% as the answer. Sometimes you may calculate an answer that has been given as a choice; it can still be incorrect. Always check your answer.

2. **b)**
   If out of the entire paycheck, 20% is first taken out, then the remainder is 80%. Of this remainder, if 30% is used for entertainment, then (.8 - .80 * .30) = .560 is left. If 10% is put into a retirement account, then (.56 - .56 * .1) = .504 is remaining. So out of $500, the part that remains is 50%, which is $252.

3. **d)**
   In 2005, the value was 1.8 times its value in 1995. So $1.8x = 7200 \rightarrow x = 4000$.

4. **c)**
   60 * (100 - 25)/100 → 60 * .75 = 45.

5. **b)**
   New price = original price * (1 – discount) → new price = 70(1-.3) = 49.

6. **c)**
   Value_{2000} = Original price * (1-.6) → 2500 = .4P = 2500 → P = 6250.

7. **b)**
   Amount = $P(1 + r)^t = 500 * 1.05^3$ = $578.81.

8. **e)**
   Final value = $75000(1 - .1)^2 = 73507$.

9. **b)**
   If the original price of the dress was x, then the discounted price would be $0.8x$. To increase the price from $.8x$ to x, the percent increase would be $(x - .8x)/.8x * 100 = 25\%$.

10. **a)**
    Let the original price of the car be x. After the 30% increase, the price is $1.3x$.

    After discounting the increased price by 30%, it now is $.7 * 1.3x = .91x$.

    Therefore, the ratio of the final price to the original price = $.91x : x$.

Test Your Knowledge: Mean, Median, Mode

1. If test A is taken 5 times with an average result of 21, and test B is taken 13 times with an average result of 23, what is the combined average?
   a) 22.24.
   b) 22.22.
   c) 22.00.
   d) 22.44.
   e) 24.22.

2. A set of data has 12 entries. The average of the first 6 entries is 12, the average of the next two entries is 20, and the average of the remaining entries is 4. What is the average of the entire data set?
   a) 10.
   b) 10.67.
   c) 11.
   d) 12.67.
   e) 10.5.

3. What is the average score of 8 tests where the score for 3 tests is 55, the score for two tests is 35, and the remaining tests have scores of 70?
   a) 50.3.
   b) 52.5.
   c) 55.1.
   d) 56.0.
   e) 55.6.

4. The temperatures over a week are recorded as follows:

Day	High	Low
Monday	80	45
Tuesday	95	34
Wednesday	78	47
Thursday	79	55
Friday	94	35
Saturday	67	46
Sunday	76	54

   What is the approximate average high temperature and average low temperature during the week?
   a) 90, 50.
   b) 80, 40.
   c) 81, 45.
   d) 82, 46.
   e) 81, 47.

5. Twelve teams competed in a mathematics test. The scores recorded for each team are: 29, 30, 28, 27, 35, 43, 45, 50, 46, 37, 44, and 41. What is the median score?

a) 37.
b) 41.
c) 39.
d) 44.
e) 45.

6. A class of 10 students scores 90, 78, 45, 98, 84, 79, 66, 87, 78, and 94. What is the mean score? What is the median score? What is the mode?

a) 69.9, 81.5, 78.
b) 79.9, 80, 78.
c) 79.9, 87, 76.
d) Not enough information given.
e) None of the above.

7. A shop sells 3 kinds of t-shirts: one design sells for $4.50, the second for $13.25, and the third for $15.50. If the shop sold 8 shirts of the first design, 12 shirts of the second design, and 4 shirts of the third design, what was the average selling price of the shirts?

a) $10.71.
b) $10.25.
c) $14.55.
d) $12.55.
e) $5.80.

Test Your Knowledge: Mean, Median, Mode – Answers

1. **d)**
   If test A avg = 21 for 5 tests, then sum of test A results = 21 * 5 = 105.
   If test B avg = 23 for 13 tests, then sum of test B results = 23 * 13 = 299.
   So total result = 299 + 105 = 404.
   Average of all tests = 404/(5 + 13) = 404/18 = 22.44.

2. **b)**
   The average of the first 6 points is 12 → $s_1/6 = 12$ → $s_1 = 72$; s_1 is the sum of the first 6 points.

   The average of the next 2 points is 20 → $s_2/2 = 20$ → $s_2 = 40$; s_2 is the sum of the next 2 points.

   The average of the remaining 4 points is 4 → $s_3/4 = 4$ → $s_3 = 16$; s_3 is the sum of the last 4 points.

   The sum of all the data points = 72 + 40 + 16 = 128.

   The average = 128/12 = 10.67.

3. **e)**
   Average = (3 * 55 + 2 * 35 + 3 * 70)/8 → Average = 55.625.

4. **c)**
   Average of high *s* = (80 + 95 + 78 + 79 + 94 + 67 + 76)/7 = 81.29.

   Average of low *s* = (45 + 34 + 47 + 55 + 35 + 46 + 54)/7 = 45.14.

5. **c)**
   To find the median, we first have to put the list in order:

   27, 28, 29, 30, 35, 37, 41, 43, 44, 45, 46, 50.

   The middle two scores are 37 and 41, and their average is 39.

6. **e) None of the above**
   The mean is just the total score/number of scores → 90 +… + 94)/10 → 79.9.

   The median is the score located in the middle. The middle of the set of the numbers is between 84 and 79. The average of these two scores is 81.5.

   The mode is the number that occurs the most: 78.

7. **a)**
   Multiply each t-shirt price with the number sold; add them together and divide by the total number of shirts sold.

   So Average Price = (4.50 * 8 + 13.25 * 12 + 15.50 * 4)/(8 + 12 + 4) → $10.71.

Test Your Knowledge: Exponents and Roots

1. What is $x^2y^3z^5/y^2z^{-9}$?
   a) y^5z^4.
   b) yz^4.
   c) x^2yz^{14}.
   d) $x^2y^5z^4$.
   e) xyz.

2. What is k if $(2m^3)^5 = 32m^{k+1}$?
   a) 11.
   b) 12.
   c) 13.
   d) 14.
   e) 15.

3. What is $x^5y^4z^3/x^{-3}y^2z^{-4}$?
   a) $x^6y^4z^7$.
   b) x^8yz^7.
   c) x^6yz^7.
   d) $x^8y^2z^7$.
   e) $x^6y^2z^7$.

4. Evaluate $(a^2 * a^{54} + a^{56} + (a^{58}/a^2))/a^4$.
   a) a^{56}.
   b) $3a^{56}$.
   c) $3a^{52}$.
   d) $3a^{54}$.
   e) a^{54}.

5. $9^m = 3^{-1/n}$. What is mn?
   a) .5.
   b) 2.
   c) -2.
   d) -.5.
   e) -1.

6. If $2^a*4^a = 32$, what is a?
   a) 1/3.
   b) 2/3.
   c) 1.
   d) 4/3.
   e) 5/3.

Test Your Knowledge: Exponents and Roots – Answers

1. **c)**
$x^2y^3z^5/y^2z^{-9} = x^2y^3z^5 * y^{-2}z^9$ which gives the answer $x^2y^{(3-2)}z^{(5+9)} \rightarrow x^2yz^{14}$.

2. **d)**
Expand $(2m^3)^5$ to give $32m^{15}$.

So$32m^{15} = 32m^{k+1} \rightarrow k+1 = 15 \rightarrow k = 14$.

3. **d)**
$x^5y^4z^3/x^{-3}y^2z^{-4} = x^5y^4z^3 * x^3y^{-2}z^4 = x^8y^2z^7$.

4. **c)**
$(a^2*a^{54}+a^{56}+ (a^{58}/a^2))/a^4 = (a^{54}+2+a^{56}+a^{58}-2)a^{-4} = 3a^{56}-4 = 3a^{52}$.

5. **d)**
9^m is the same as 3^{2m}.

So $3^{2m} = 3^{-1/n} \rightarrow 2m = -1/n \rightarrow mn = -.5$.

6. **e)**
$2^a * 4^a$ can be re-written as $2^a * (2^2)^a$.

$32 = 2^5$.

Therefore, $2^{(a+2a)} = 2^5 \rightarrow 3a = 5 \rightarrow a = 5/3$.

Test Your Knowledge: Algebraic Equations

1. The number 568*cd* should be divisible by 2, 5, and 7. What are the values of the digits *c* and *d*?
   a) 56835.
   b) 56830.
   c) 56860.
   d) 56840.
   e) 56800.

2. Carla is 3 times older than her sister Megan. Eight years ago, Carla was 18 years older than her sister. What is Megan's age?
   a) 10.
   b) 8.
   c) 9.
   d) 6.
   e) 5.

3. What is the value of $f(x) = (x^2 - 25)/(x + 5)$ when $x = 0$?
   a) -1.
   b) -2.
   c) -3.
   d) -4.
   e) -5.

4. Four years from now, John will be twice as old as Sally will be. If Sally was 10 eight years ago, how old is John?
   a) 35.
   b) 40.
   c) 45.
   d) 50.
   e) 55.

5. I have some marbles. I give 25% to Vic, 20% to Robbie, 10% to Jules. I then give 6/20 of the remaining amount to my brother, and keep the rest for myself. If I end up with 315 marbles, how many did I have to begin with?
   a) 1000.
   b) 1500.
   c) 3500.
   d) 400.
   e) 500.

6. I have some marbles. I give 25% to Vic, 20% of the remainder to Robbie, 10% of that remainder to Jules and myself I then give 6/20 of the remaining amount to my brother, and keep the rest for myself. If I end up with 315 marbles, how many did I have to begin with?
   a) 800.
   b) 833.
   c) 834.
   d) 378.
   e) 500.

7. If $x = 5y + 4$, what is the value of y if $x = 29$?
   a) 33/5.
   b) 5.5.
   c) 5.
   d) 0.
   e) 29/5.

8. A bag of marbles has 8 marbles. If I buy 2 bags of marbles, how many more bags of marbles would I need to buy to have a total of at least 45 marbles?
   a) 3.
   b) 4.
   c) 5.
   d) 6.
   e) 29.

9. A factory that produces widgets wants to sell them each for $550. It costs $50 for the raw materials for each widget, and the startup cost for the factory was $10000. How many widgets have to be sold so that the factory can break even?
   a) 10.
   b) 20.
   c) 30.
   d) 40.
   e) 50.

10. Expand $(3x - 4)(6 - 2x)$.
   a) $6x^2 - 6x + 8$.
   b) $-6x^2 + 26x - 24$.
   c) $6x^2 - 26x + 24$.
   d) $-6x^2 + 26x + 24$.
   e) $6x^2 + 26x - 24$.

11. If $6n + m$ is divisible by 3 and 5, which of the following numbers when added to $6n + m$ will still give a result that is divisible by 3 and 5?
   a) 4.
   b) 6.
   c) 12.
   d) 20.
   e) 60.

12. If x is negative, and $x^3/5$ and $x/5$ both give the same result, what could be the value of x?
   a) -5.
   b) -4.
   c) 3.
   d) 0.
   e) -1.

13. If $m = 3548$, and $n = 235$, then what is the value of $m * n$?

a) 87940.
b) 843499.
c) 87900.
d) 8830.
e) 833780.

14. A ball is thrown at a speed of 30 mph. How far will it travel in 2 minutes and 35 seconds?

a) 1.5 miles.
b) 1.20 miles.
c) 1.29 miles.
d) 1.3 miles.
e) 1.1 miles.

15. Simplify: $30(\sqrt{40} - \sqrt{60})$.

a) $30(\sqrt{5} - \sqrt{15})$.
b) $30(\sqrt{10} + \sqrt{15})$.
c) $60(\sqrt{5} + \sqrt{15})$.
d) $60(\sqrt{10} - \sqrt{15})$.
e) 60.

16. Simplify: $30/(\sqrt{40} - \sqrt{60})$.

a) $3(\sqrt{5} + \sqrt{15})$.
b) $-3(\sqrt{5} - \sqrt{15})$.
c) $-3(\sqrt{10} + \sqrt{15})$.
d) $3(\sqrt{10} + \sqrt{15})$.
e) $3(\sqrt{10} - \sqrt{15})$.

17. What is the least common multiple of 2, 3, 4, and 5?

a) 30.
b) 60.
c) 120.
d) 40.
e) 50.

18. It costs \$6 to make a pen that sells for \$12. How many pens need to be sold to make a profit of \$60?

a) 10.
b) 6.
c) 72.
d) 30.
e) 12.

Test Your Knowledge: Algebraic Equations – Answers

1. **d)**
   If the number is divisible by 2, d should be even. If the number is divisible by 5, then b has to equal 0.

   Start by making both variables 0 and dividing by the largest factor, 7.

   56800/7 = 8114.

   2 from 56800 is 56798, a number divisible by 2 and 7.

   Next add a multiple of 7 that turns the last number to a 0. 6 * 7 = 42. 56798 + 42 = 56840, which is divisible by 2, 5, and 7.

2. **c)**
   Carla's age is c; Megan's age is m. $c = 3m$; $c - 8 = m - 8 + 18$.

   Substitute $3m$ for c in equation 2 → $3m - 8 = m + 10$ → $m = 9$.

3. **e)**
   We know $(x^2 - 25) = (x + 5)(x - 5)$.

   So $(x^2 - 25)/(x + 5) = x - 5$. At $x = 0$, $f(0) = -5$.

4. **b)**
   Let j be John's age and s be Sally's age.

   $j + 4 = 2(s + 4)$.

   $s - 8 = 10$ → $s = 18$.

   So $j + 4 = 2(18 + 4)$ → $j = 40$.

5. **a)**
   If x is the number of marbles initially, then $.25x$ goes to Vic, $.2x$ goes to Robbie, and $.1x$ goes to Jules.

   The number left, x, is $(1 - .25 - .2 - .1) = .45x$.

   Of that I give 6/20 to my brother, so $6/20 * .45x$.

   I am left with $.45x(1 - (6/20)) = .315x$.

   We are also told $.315x = 315$ → $x = 1000$.

6. c)

Always read the question carefully! Questions 5 and 6 are similar, but they are not the same.

Let x be the original number of marbles. After Vic's share is given $.75x$ remains. After Robbie's share $.75x * .80$ remains. After Jules' share, $.75x * .8 * .9$ remains.

After I give my brother his share, $.75x * .8 * .9 * (1 - 6/20)$ remains. The remaining number = $.378x$.

We are told $.378x = 315 \rightarrow x = 833.33$. We need to increase this to the next highest number, 834, because we have part of a marble and to include it we need to have a whole marble.

7. c)

Replace the value of x with its value and solve the equation.

$29 = 5y + 4$.

Solving:

$29 - 4 = 5y + 4 - 4$.

$25 = 5y$ or $5y = 25$.

$5y/5 = 25/5$.

$y = 5$.

8. b)

$2(8) + x > 45$ means $x > 29$, so we need more than 29 marbles. A bag has 8 marbles, so the number of bags needed is 29/8, or 3.625. Since we need 3 bags + part of another bag, we need 4 additional bags to give at least 45 marbles.

9. b)

n is the number of widgets. The cost the factory incurs for making n widgets is $10000 + 50n$. The amount the factory makes by selling n widgets is $550n$.

At the break-even point, the cost incurred is equal to the amount of sales.

$10000 + 50n = 550n \rightarrow n = 20$.

10. b)

Use FOIL:

$(3x - 4)(6 - 2x) = 3x * 6 - 4 * 6 + 3x * (-2x) - 4 * (-2x) = 18x - 24 - 6x^2 + 8x = -6x^2 + 26x - 24$.

11. e)

Since $6n + m$ is divisible by 3 and 5, the new number that we get after adding a value will be divisible by 3 and 5 only if the value that we add is divisible by 3 and 5. The only number that will work from the given choices is 60.

12. e)

We are told $x^3/5 = x/5 \rightarrow x^3 = x$. The possible values are -1, 0, and 1. We are told that x is negative.

So $x = -1$.

13. e)

This problem can be done by elimination. We know that m is in the thousands, which means $x * 10^3$; and n is in the hundreds, which is $y * 10^2$. The answer will be $z * 10^5$, or 6 places in total, so we can eliminate **a)**, **c)**, and **d)**. Also we see that m ends in 8 and n ends in 5, so the answer has to end in 0 (8 * 5 = 40), which eliminates **b)**.

14. c)

The ball has a speed of 30 miles per hour. 30 miles per 60 minutes = .5 mile per minute; 2 minutes and 35 seconds = 2 minutes; and 35/60 minutes = 2.58 minutes.

The ball travels .5 * 2.58 = 1.29 miles.

15. d)

$30(\sqrt{40} - \sqrt{60}) = 30\sqrt{4\,(10-15)} = 60(\sqrt{10} - \sqrt{15})$.

16. c)

Multiply the numerator and the denominator by $(\sqrt{40} + \sqrt{60})$.

So $30/(\sqrt{40} - \sqrt{60}) * [(\sqrt{40} + \sqrt{60})/(\sqrt{40} + \sqrt{60})] = 30(\sqrt{40} + \sqrt{60})/(\sqrt{40} - \sqrt{60})^2$.

$-3(\sqrt{10} + \sqrt{15})$.

17. b)

Find all the prime numbers that multiply to give the numbers.

For 2, prime factor is 2; for 3, prime factor is 3; for 4, prime factors are 2, 2; and for 5, prime factor is 5. Note the maximum times of occurrence of each prime and multiply these to find the least common multiple.

The LCM is 2 * 2 * 3 * 5 = 60.

18. a)

One pen sells for $12, so on the sale of a pen, the profit is 12 - 6 = 6.

In order to make $60, we need to sell 10 pens.

Test Your Knowledge: Inequalities, Literal Equations, Polynomials, and Binomials

1. If $x < 5$ and $y < 6$, then $x + y$ __?__ 11.

a) $<$
b) $>$
c) $\leq$
d) $\geq$
e) $=$

2. Which of the following is true about the inequality $25x^2 - 40x - 32 < 22$?

a) There are no solutions.
b) There is a set of solutions.
c) There is 1 solution only.
d) There are 2 solutions.
e) There are 3 solutions.

3. If $x - 2y > 6$, what possible values of y always have x as greater than or equal to 2?

a) $y \geq 1$.
b) $y \leq 0$.
c) $y \geq -2$.
d) $y < 2$.
e) $y \leq 6$.

4. Find the point of intersection of the lines $x + 2y = 4$ and $3x - y = 26$.

a) (1, 3).
b) (8, -2).
c) (0, 2).
d) (2, -1).
e) (4, 26).

5. If $a + b = 2$, and $a - b = 4$, what is a?

a) 1.
b) 2.
c) 3.
d) 4.
e) 5.

6. If $\sqrt{a} + \sqrt{b} = 2$, and $\sqrt{a} - \sqrt{b} = 3$, what is $a + b$?

a) 6.5.
b) 6.
c) 5.5.
d) 5.
e) 4.5.

7. If $a = b + 3$, and $3b = 5a + 6$, what is $3a - 2b$?

a) -1.5.
b) 2.5.
c) 3.
d) 4.3.
e) 5.

8. The sum of the roots of a quadratic equation is 8, and the difference is 2. What is the equation?

a) $x^2 - 8x - 15$.
b) $x^2 + 8x + 15$.
c) $x^2 - 8x + 15$.
d) $x^2 + 8x - 15$.
e) $x^2 + 15$.

9. Solve the following system of equations: $3x + 2y = 7$ and $3x + y = 5$.

a) $x = 2, y = 1$.
b) $x = 2, y = 2$.
c) $x = 1, y = 0$.
d) $x = 1, y = 2$.
e) $x = 1, y = 1$.

10. Nine tickets were sold for $41. If the tickets cost $4 and $5, how many $5 tickets were sold?

a) 5.
b) 4.
c) 9.
d) 6.
e) 7.

11. Joe brought a bag of 140 M&Ms to his class of 40 students. Each boy received 2 M&Ms. Each girl received 4. How many boys were in the class?

a) 10.
b) 20.
c) 30.
d) 40.
e) 50.

Test Your Knowledge: Inequalities, Literal Equations, Polynomials, and Binomials – Answers

1. **a)**
   Choice **a)** will always be true, while the other choices can never be true.

2. **b)**
   $25x^2 - 40x + 32 < 22 \rightarrow 25x^2 - 40x + 16 < 6 \rightarrow (5x - 4)^2 < 6 \rightarrow 5x - 4 < 6$.

   $x = 2$, so x has to be all numbers less than 2 for this inequality to work.

3. **c)**
   Rearrange equation $x > 6 + 2y$, so $2 > 6 + 2y$. Solve for y.

   $2 \geq 6 + 2y$.

   $-4 \geq 2y$, so $-2 \leq y$ or $y \geq -2$.

   (When working with inequalities, remember to reverse the sign when dividing by a negative number.)

4. **b)**
   Find the slopes first. If they are not equal, then the lines intersect. The slopes are -1/2 and 3.

   Next, solve by substitution or addition. From the first equation, $x = 4 - 2y$. Plugging this into equation 2, we get $3(4 - 2y) - y = 26 \rightarrow 7y = 12 - 26 \rightarrow y = -2$. Plug this value into either equation to find x.

   With equation 1, we get $x - 4 = 4 \rightarrow x = 8$.

5. **c)**

   Add the equations to eliminate b. $2a = 6 \rightarrow a = 3$.

6. **a)**
   Square both equations.

   Equation 1 becomes $a + 2\sqrt{ab} + b = 4$; and equation 2 becomes $a - 2\sqrt{ab} + b = 9$.

   Add the equations.
   $2(a + b) = 13 \rightarrow a + b = 13/2$. $13/2 = 6.5$.

7. a)
Solve by substitution.

If $a = b + 3$, and $3b = 5a + 6$, then $3b = 5(b+3) + 6$.

If $3b - 5b - 15 = 6$, then $-2b = 21$. Therefore, $b = -10.5$.

Now use substitution to find a.

$a = b + 3$. So $a = -10.5 + 3$. Therefore, $a = -7.5$.

Solve the equation, $3a - 2b$.

$3(-7.5) - 2(-10.5) = -1.5$.

8. c)
If the roots are a and b, then $a + b = 8$ and $a - b = 2$.

Add the equations. $2a = 10 \rightarrow a = 5 \rightarrow b = 3$.

The factors are $(x - 5)(x - 3)$, and the equation is $x^2 - 8x + 15$.

9. d)
From the equation $3x + y = 5$, we get $y = 5 - 3x$. Substitute into the other equation. $3x + 2(5 - 3x) = 7$ $\rightarrow 3x + 10 - 6x = 7 \rightarrow x = 1$. This value into either of the equations gives us $y = 2$.

10. a)
$4x + 5y = 41$, and $x + y = 9$, where x and y are the number of tickets sold.

From equation 2: $x = 9 - y$.

From equation 1: $4(9 - y) + 5y = 41 \rightarrow 36 + y = 41 \rightarrow y = 5$.

11. a)
b is the number of boys, and g is the number of girls. So $b + g = 40$, and $2b + 4g = 140$.

To do the problem, use the substitution method. Plug $(g = 40 - b)$ into $(2b + 4g = 140)$.

$2b + 4(40 - b) = 140 \rightarrow b = 10$.

Test Your Knowledge: Slope and Distance to Midpoint

1. What is the equation of the line that passes through (3, 5), with intercept $y = 8$?
   a) $y = x + 8$.
   b) $y = x - 8$.
   c) $y = -x - 8$.
   d) $y = -x + 8$.
   e) $y = -x$.

2. What is the value of y in the equation $(3x - 4)^2 = 4y - 15$, if $x = 3$?
   a) 10.
   b) 2.5.
   c) -10.
   d) -2.5.
   e) 5.

3. If $y = 4x + 6y$, what is the range of y if $-10 < x \leq 5$?
   a) $-4 < y \leq 8$.
   b) $-4 < y < 8$.
   c) $8 > y > -4$.
   d) $-4 \leq y < 8$.
   e) $-4 \leq y \leq 8$.

4. If Jennifer gets three times as much allowance as Judy gets, and Judy gets $5/week, how much does Jennifer get every month?
   a) $15.
   b) $20.
   c) $30.
   d) $45.
   e) $60.

5. What is the value of x, if $y = 8$ in the equation $5x + 9y = 3x - 6y + 5$?
   a) 57.5.
   b) 60.
   c) -60.
   d) -57.5.
   e) None of the above.

6. What is the area outside the circle, but within the square whose two corners are A and B?

A (3, 5) B (8, 17)

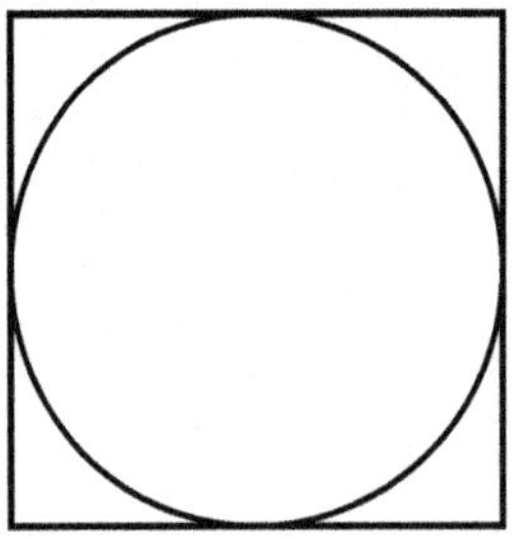

a) 169(1-π).
b) 169 π.
c) 169 π /4.
d) 169(1- π /4).
e) 169.

7. Determine where the following two lines intersect:

$$3x + 4y = 7$$
$$9x + 12y = 21$$

a) $x = 4, y = 3$.
b) $x = 12, y = 9$.
c) $x = 1/3, y = 1/3$.
d) Not enough information provided.
e) There is no solution; the lines do not intersect.

8. A line with a slope of 2 passes through the point (2, 4). What is the set of coordinates where that line passes through the y intercept?

a) (-2, 0).
b) (0, 0).
c) (2, 2).
d) (4, 0).
e) (1, 1).

9. Are the following lines parallel or perpendicular?

$$3x + 4y = 7$$
$$8x - 6y = 9$$

a) Parallel.
b) Perpendicular.
c) Neither parallel nor perpendicular.
d) Cannot be determined.
e) The angle at the point of intersection is 40.

10. Is the graph of the function $f(x) = -3x^2 + 4$ linear, asymptotical, symmetrical to the x axis, symmetrical to the y axis, or not symmetrical to either axis?

a) Symmetrical to the x axis.
b) Symmetrical to the y axis.
c) Symmetrical to neither axis.
d) Asymptotic.
e) Linear.

11. Two points on a line have coordinates (3, 12) and (9, 20). What is the distance between these two points?

a) 10.
b) 12.
c) 13.
d) 8.
e) 11.

12. In the following graph, what is the equation of line AB if line AB is perpendicular to line PQ? Point coordinates are:

M (-4, 0); O (0, 2); and N (0, -3). The lines intersect at (-2,1).

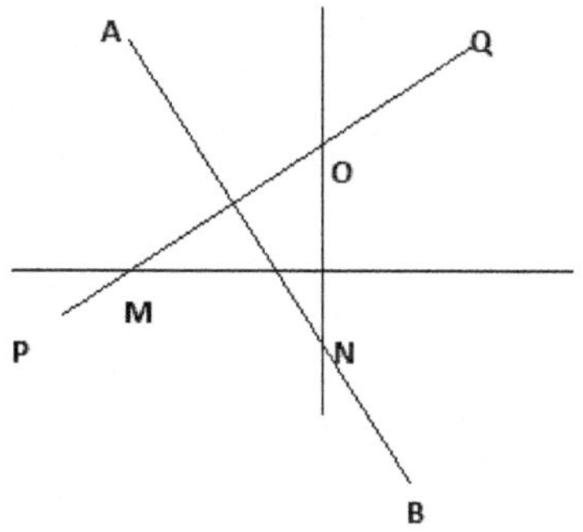

a) $y = 2x + 3$.
b) $y = -2x - 3$.
c) $y = x - 4$.
d) $y = x + 3$.
e) $y = -2x - 3$.

13. What is the equation of a line passing through (1, 2) and (6, 12)?

a) $y = x$.
b) $y = 2x$.
c) $y = x/2$.
d) $y = 2x + 2$.
e) $y = x - 2$.

14. What is the midpoint of the line connecting points (0, 8) and (2, 6)?

a) (-1, 1).
b) (2, 14).
c) (-2, 2).
d) (0, 1).
e) (1, 7).

15. What is the equation of a line passing through (1, 1) and (2, 4)?

a) $3y = x + 2$.
b) $2y = x + 3$.
c) $y = 3x - 2$.
d) $4x = y + 2$.
e) $y = (1/3)x + 2$.

16. Line A passes through (0, 0) and (3, 4). Line B passes through (2, 6) and (3, y). What value of y will make the lines parallel?

a) 20/3.
b) 7.
c) 22/3.
d) 29.
e) 5.

17. Line A passes through (1, 3) and (3, 4). Line B passes through (3, 7) and (5, y). What value of y will make the lines perpendicular?

a) 1.
b) 2.
c) 3.
d) 4.
e) 5.

18. What is the equation of line A that is perpendicular to line B, connecting (8, 1) and (10, 5), that intersects at (x, 14)?

a) $y = 2x - 7$.
b) $y = -2x + 7$.
c) $y = (-1/2)x + 19\frac{1}{4}$.
d) $y = 5x - 7$.
e) $y = 2x - 19\frac{1}{4}$.

Test Your Knowledge: Slope and Distance to Midpoint – Answers

1. **d)**
   The standard form of the line equation is $y = mx + b$. We need to find slope m.

   $m = (y_2 - y_1)/(x_2 - x_1) \rightarrow m = (5 - 8)/(3 - 0) \rightarrow m = -1$.

   Therefore the equation is $y = -x + 8$.

2. **a)**
   At $x = 3$, $((3 * 3) - 4)^2 = 4y - 15$.

   $(9 - 4)^2 = 4y - 15$.

   $25 = 4y - 15$.

   $40 = 4y$.

   $y = 10$.

3. **d)**
   Rearrange the equation and combine like terms. $-5y = 4x$.

   At $x = -10$, $y = 8$. At $x = 5$, $y = -4$. The range of y is therefore $-4 \leq y < 8$.

4. **e)**
   If Judy gets x dollars, then Jennifer gets $3x$ in a week. In a month, Jennifer will then get $4 * 3x$.

   If Judy gets \$5 per week, then Jennifer gets \$60 in a month.

5. **d)**
   Combine like terms.

   $5x + 9y = 3x - 6y + 5 \rightarrow 2x = -15y + 5 \rightarrow x = -57.5$ when $y = 8$.

6. **d)**
   First we need to find the length of side AB.

   $AB = \sqrt{(17 - 5)^2 + (8 - 3)^2} = 13$.

   If AB = 13, then $A_{square} = 13^2 = 169$.

   AB is also the diameter of the circle. $A_{circle}\ \pi\ (d^2/4) = 169\ \pi/4$.

   The area outside the circle and within the square is: $A_{square} - A_{circle} = 169(1 - \pi/4)$.

7. e)

While it is tempting to solve this system of simultaneous equations to find the values of x and y, the first thing to do is to see whether the lines intersect. To do this, compare the slopes of the two lines by putting the lines into the standard form, $y = mx + b$, where m is the slope.

By rearranging, equation 1 becomes $y = 7/4 - 3x/4$; and equation 2 becomes $y = 21/12 - 9x/12$.

The slope of line 1 is -3/4, and the slope of line 2 is -9/12, which reduces to -3/4. Since the slopes are equal, the lines are parallel and do not intersect.

8. b)

The slope of the line is given as $m = (y_2 - y_1)/(x_2 - x_1)$, where (x_1, y_1) and (x_2, y_2) are two points which the line passes through.

The y intercept is the point where the graph intersects the y axis, so $x = 0$ at this point.

Plug in the values of m, etc.; we get $2 = (4 - y)/(2 - 0) \rightarrow y = 0$.

9. b)

Find the slopes by rearranging the two equations into the form $y = mx + b$.

Equation 1 becomes $y = -3x/4 + 7/4$ and equation 2 becomes $y = 8x/6 - 9/6$.

So $m_1 = -3/4$ and $m_2 = 8/6 = 4/3$. We see that m_1 is the negative inverse of m_2, so line 1 is perpendicular to line 2.

10. b)

Find the values of the y coordinate for different values of the x coordinate (example, [-3, +3]). We get the following chart:

x	y
-3	-23
-2	-8
-1	1
0	4
1	1
2	-8
3	-23

From these values, we see the graph is symmetrical to the y axis.

11. a)

Distance $s = \sqrt{(x_2 - x_1)^2 + (y_2 - y_1)^2} \rightarrow s = \sqrt{(9 - 3)^2 + (20 - 12)^2} = \sqrt{36 + 64} = 10$.

12. b)

$y = mx + b$; m is the slope and b is the y intercept.

Calculate m for line AB using the given points (0, -3) and (-2, 1). $m = (-3 -1)/(0-(-2)) = -2$. The y intercept is -3 (from point set given), so $y = -2x - 3$.

13. b)

First, find the slope, $(y_2-y_1)/(x_2-x_1)$ → slope = (12 - 2)/(6 - 1) = 2.

Next, use the slope and a point to find the value of b.

In the standard line equation, $y = mx + b$, use the point (6, 12) to get 12 = (2 * 6) + b → $b = 0$.

The equation of the line is $y = 2x$.

14. e)

The midpoint is at $(x_1 + x_2)/2,(y_1 + y_2)/2$ = (1,7).

15. c)

Slope = $(y_2 - y_1)/(x_2 - x_1)$ = 3. Plug one of the coordinates into $y = mx + b$ to find the value of b.

1 = 3(1) + b → b = - 2.

The equation of the line is $y = 3x - 2$.

16. c)

Calculate the slope of each line. Slope of line A = 4/3; and slope of line B = y - 6.

The slopes of the line have to be the same for the lines to be parallel.

$4/3 = y - 6$ → $4 = 3y - 18$ → $y = 22/3$.

17. c)

The slope of line A = ½; and the slope of line B = $(y - 7)/2$.

The product of the slopes has to equal -1.

$(1/2)[(y - 7)/2] = -1$ → $(y - 7)/4 = -1$ → $y = 3$.

18. c)

Slope_b = (5 - 1)/(10 - 8) = 2. The slope of line A is -1/2.

To find the intercept of line B, use $y = mx + b$.

5 = (2)(10) + b, so b = -7. Equation of line B is $y = 2x - 7$.

Find intersect x, using the given y coordinate. $14 = 2x - 7$; $x = 10.5$.

Find the intercept of line A using the coordinates of intersection.

$14 = (-1/2)(10.5)+b$. $b = 19\frac{1}{4}$.

The equation of line A is $y = -(1/2)x + 19\frac{1}{4}$.

Test Your Knowledge: Absolute Value Equations

1. Factor $x^2 + 2x - 15$.
   a) $(x - 3)(x + 5)$.
   b) $(x + 3)(x - 5)$.
   c) $(x + 3)(x + 5)$.
   d) $(x - 3)(x - 5)$.
   e) $(x - 1)(x + 15)$.

2. Car A starts at 3:15 PM and travels straight to its destination at a constant speed of 50 mph. If it arrives at 4:45 PM, how far did it travel?
   a) 70 miles.
   b) 75 miles.
   c) 65 miles.
   d) 40 miles.
   e) 105 miles.

3. What are the roots of the equation $2x^2 + 14x = 0$?
   a) 0 and 7.
   b) 0 and -7.
   c) 14 and 0.
   d) 2 and 14.
   e) Cannot be determined.

4. If $f(x) = 2x^2 + 3x$, and $g(x) = x + 4$, what is $f[g(x)]$?
   a) $x^2 + 19x + 44$.
   b) $2x^2 + 19x + 44$.
   c) $4x^2 + 35x + 76$.
   d) $x^2 + 8x + 16$.
   e) None of the above.

5. If $|x + 4| = 2$, what are the values of x?
   a) 2 and 6.
   b) -2 and -6.
   c) -2.
   d) -6.
   e) 0.

6. The sale of an item can be written as a function of price: $s = 3p + c$, where s is the amount in sales, p is the price charged per item, and c is a constant value. If the sales generated are \$20 at a price of \$5 for the item, then what should the price be to generate \$50 in sales?
   a) \$10.
   b) \$15.
   c) \$20.
   d) \$16.
   e) \$14.

7. If $f(n) = 2n + 3\sqrt{n}$, where n is a positive integer, what is f[g(5)] if $g(m) = m - 4$?

a) 1.
b) 2.
c) 3.
d) 4.
e) 5.

8. If $f(x) = (x + 2)^2$, and $-4 \leq x \leq 4$, what is the minimum value of f(x)?

a) 0.
b) 1.
c) 2.
d) 3.
e) 4.

9. If $f(x) = (x + 2)^2$, and $0 \leq x \leq 4$, what is the minimum value of f(x)?

a) 1.
b) 2.
c) 3.
d) 4.
e) 5.

10. What is $x^2 - 9$ divided by $x - 3$?

a) $x - 3$.
b) $x + 3$.
c) x.
d) $x - 1$.
e) 6.

11. An equation has two roots: 5 and -8. What is a possible equation?

a) $x^2 - 3x + 40$.
b) $x^2 - 3x - 40$.
c) $x^2 + x + 40$.
d) $x^2 + 3x - 40$.
e) $2x^2 - 3x + 40$.

12. In an ant farm, the number of ants grows every week according to the formula $N = 100 + 2^w$, where w is the number of weeks elapsed. How many ants will the colony have after 5 weeks?

a) 115.
b) 125.
c) 135.
d) 132.
e) 233.

13. Find the values of x that validate the following equation: $[(4x + 5)^2 - (40x + 25)]^{1/2} + 3|x| - 14 = 0$.

a) -2, -14.
b) 2, -14.
c) -2, 14.
d) 2, 14.
e) No solution.

14. If $|x| = 4$ and $|y| = 5$, what are the values of $|x + y|$?

a) 1, 9.
b) -1, 9.
c) -1, -9.
d) -1, -9.
e) $1 < |x + y| < 9$.

15. If $y = |x|$, what is the range of y?

a) $y < 0$.
b) $0 < y < \text{x}$.
c) $y > 0$.
d) $y \geq 0$.
e) $y > x$.

Test Your Knowledge: Absolute Value Equations – Answers

1. **a)**
The constant term is -15. The factors should multiply to give -15 and add to give 2.
The numbers -3 and 5 satisfy both, $(x - 3)(x + 5)$.

2. **b)**
The time between 3:15 PM and 4:45 PM = 1.5 hours. 1.5 * 50 = 75.

Reminder: half an hour is written as .5 of an hour, not .3 of an hour, even though on a clock a half hour is 30 minutes.

3. **b)**
Rearrange, reduce, and factor.

$2x^2 + 14x + 0 = 0.$

$2(x^2 + 7x + 0) = 0.$

$(x + 7)\ (x + 0).$

$x = 0$, or -7.

4. **b)**
Substitute g(x) for every x in f(x).

$f[g((x + 4))] = 2(x + 4)^2 + 3(x + 4) = 2x^2 + 16x + 32 + 3x + 12 = 2x^2 + 19x + 44.$

5. **b)**
Two solutions: $(x + 4) = 2$ and $-(x + 4) = 2$.

Or $x + 4 = 2, x = -2$.

And $x + 4 = -2, x = -6$.

6. **b)**
Find the value of the constant by plugging in the given information.

$20 = 3 * 5 + c \rightarrow c = 5.$

Now use the value of c and the new value of s to find p.$50 = 3p + 5 \rightarrow p = 15$.

7. **e)**
$g(5) = 5 - 4 = 1$. $f[g(5)] = 2 * 1 + 3\sqrt{1} = 5$.

8. **a)**
From the domain of x, the lowest value of x is -4, and the highest value is 4. We are tempted to think that f(x) will have the least value at $x = -4$: f(-4) = 4. However, f(x) is equal to a squared value, so the lowest value of f(x) is 0. This happens at $x = -2$.

9. d)

The lowest value of $f(x)$ can be 0, since $f(x)$ is equal to a squared value, but, for $f(x) = 0$, x must equal -2. That is outside the domain of x. The least value of $f(x) = 4$.

10. b)

$x^2 - 9$ can be factored into $(x + 3)$ and $(x - 3)$.

$[(x + 3)(x - 3)]/(x - 3) = x + 3$.

11. d)

If the roots are 5 and -8, then the factors are $(x - 5)(x + 8)$. Multiply the factors to get the equation.

$x^2 + 3x - 40$.

12. d)

After 5 weeks, the number of ants = 100 + 32, or 132.

13. d)

Expand the equation:

$[16x^2 + 40x + 25 - 40x - 25]^{1/2} + 3|x| - 14 = 0$.

$(16x^2)^{1/2} + 3|x| - 14 = 0$.

$4x + 3|x| - 14 = 0$.

$3|x| = 14 - 4x$.

$|x| = \frac{14}{3} - \frac{4x}{3}$ $\quad x = \frac{14}{3} - \frac{4x}{3} = 2$ $\quad x = -\frac{14}{3} - \frac{4x}{3} = 14$.

14. a)

$x = 4$ and $y = 5$, $|x + y| = 9$.

$x = -4$ and $y = 5$, $|x + y| = 1$.

$x = 4$ and $y = -5$, $|x + y| = 1$.

$x = -4$ and $y = -5$, $|x + y| = 9$.

15. d)

The absolute value of x can be at least a 0, and is otherwise positive regardless of the value of x.

$y \geq 0$.

Test Your Knowledge: Geometry

1. What is the area, in square feet, of the triangle whose sides have lengths equal to 3, 4, and 5 feet?

a) 6 square feet.
b) 7 square feet.
c) 4 square feet.
d) 5 square feet.
e) 8 square feet.

2. In the following figure, where AE bisects line BC, and angles AEC and AEB are both right angles, what is the length of AB?

a) 1 cm.
b) 2 cm.
c) 3 cm.
d) 4 cm.
e) 5 cm.

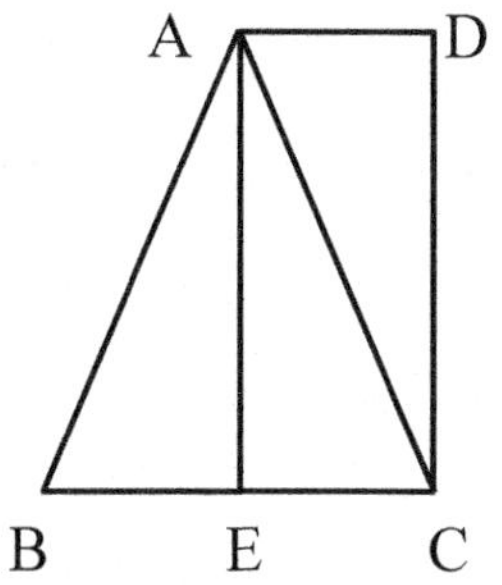

BC = 6 cm
AD = 3 cm
CD = 4 cm

3. In the following triangle, if AB = 6 and BC = 8, what should the length of CA be to make triangle ABC a right triangle?

a) 10.
b) 9.
c) 8.
d) 4.
e) 7.

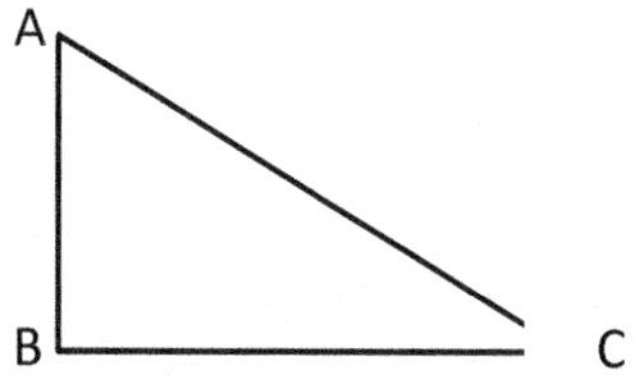

4. In the following circle there is a square with an area of 36 cm^2. What is the area outside the square, but within the circle?

a) 18π cm^2.
b) 18π - 30 cm^2.
c) 18π - 36 cm^2.
d) 18 cm^2.
e) -18 cm^2.

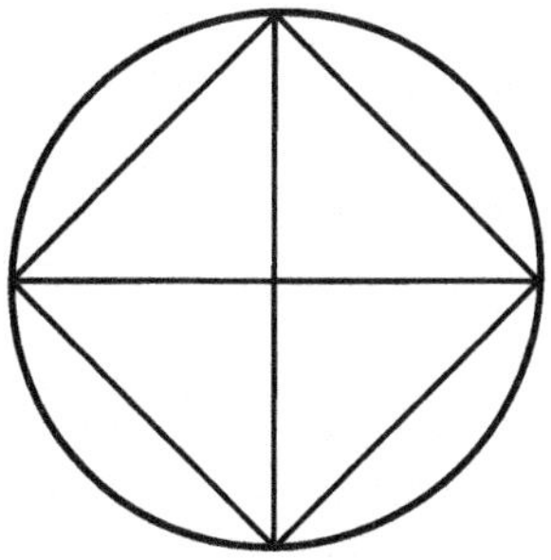

5. The length of a rectangle is 4 times its width. If the width of the rectangle is 5 - x inches, and the perimeter of the rectangle is 30 inches, what is x?
   a) 1.
   b) 2.
   c) 3.
   d) 4.
   e) 5.

6. Two sides of a triangle have a ratio AC:BC = 5:4. The length of AB on a similar triangle = 24. What is the actual value of AC for the larger triangle?
   a) 10.
   b) 14.4.
   c) 35.
   d) 40.
   e) 50.

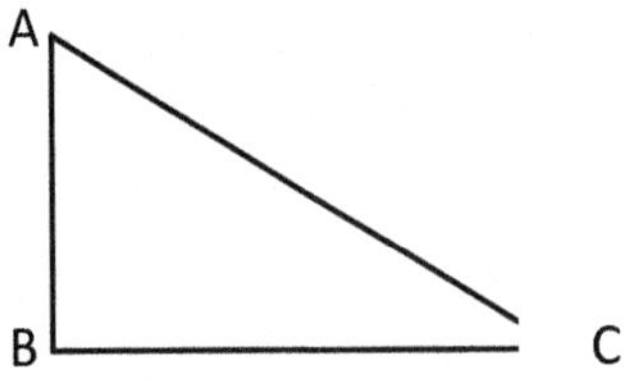

7. If the diameter of a circle is doubled, the area increases by what factor?
   a) 1 time.
   b) 2 times.
   c) 3 times.
   d) 4 times.
   e) 5 times.

8. In the following triangle PQR, what is the measure of angle A?
   a) 145^0.
   b) 140^0.
   c) 70^0.
   d) 50^0.
   e) 40^0.

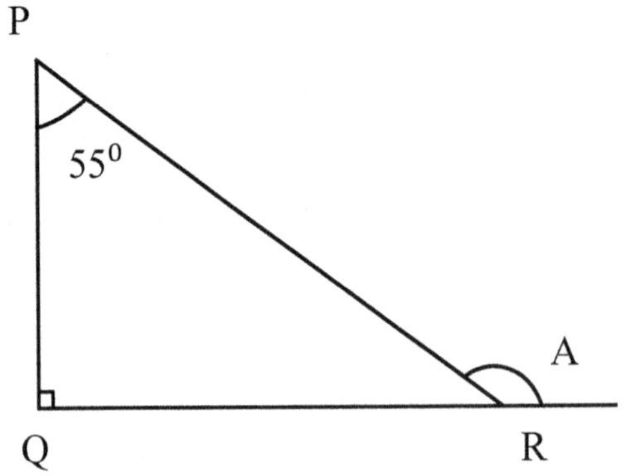

Test Your Knowledge: Geometry – Answers

1. a)
The Pythagorean triple (special right triangle property) means the two shorter sides form a right triangle.

$1/2bh = A$. So, $(1/2)(3)(4) = 6$.

2. e)
$AB^2 = AC^2 = AD2 + CD^2 \rightarrow AB^2 = 3^2 + 4^2 \rightarrow AB = 5$.

3. a)
In a right triangle, the square of the hypotenuse = the sum of the squares of the other two sides.

$AB^2 + BC^2 = AC^2 \rightarrow AC^2 = 36 + 64 \rightarrow AC = 10$.

4. c)
If the area of the square is 36 cm^2, then each side is 6 cm. If we look at the triangle made by half the square, that diagonal would be the hypotenuse of the triangle, and its length = $\sqrt{6^2 + 6^2} = 6\sqrt{2}$.

This hypotenuse is also the diameter of the circle, so the radius of the circle is $3\sqrt{2}$.

The area of the circle = $A = \pi r^2 = 18\pi$.

The area outside the square, but within the circle is $18\pi - 36$.

5. b)
Perimeter of a rectangle = $2(l + w)$. Width = $5 - x$; and length = $4(5 - x)$.

Perimeter = $2(l * w) = 30 \rightarrow 2(20 - 4x + 5 - x) = 30 \rightarrow -10x = -20 \rightarrow x = 2$.

6. d)
Side AC = 5, and side BC = 4. The Pythagorean triple is 3:4:5, so side AB = 3.

Because the other triangle is similar, the ratio of all sides is constant. AB:AB = 3:24. The ratio factor is 8.

AC of the larger triangle = 5 * 8 = 40.

7. d)
The area of a circle = πr^2.

If the diameter is doubled, then the radius is also doubled.

The new area = $\pi * (2r)^2 = 4 * \pi * r^2$. The area increases four times.

8. a)
$\angle P = 55^0$. $\angle Q = 90^0$. $\angle R = 180 - (55 + 90) = 35^0$, and $\angle A = 180 - 35 = 145^0$.

Test Your Knowledge: Fundamental Counting Principle, Permutations, Combinations

1. The wardrobe of a studio contains 4 hats, 3 suits, 5 shirts, 2 pants, and 3 pairs of shoes. How many different ways can these items be put together?

a) 60.
b) 300.
c) 360.
d) 420.
e) 500.

2. For lunch, you have a choice between chicken fingers or cheese sticks for an appetizer; turkey, chicken, or veal for the main course; cake or pudding for dessert; and either Coke or Pepsi for a beverage. How many choices of possible meals do you have?

a) 16.
b) 24.
c) 34.
d) 36.
e) 8.

3. For an office job, I need to pick 3 candidates out of a pool of 5. How many choices do I have?

a) 60.
b) 20.
c) 10.
d) 30.
e) 50.

4. A contractor is supposed to choose 3 tiles out of a stack of 5 tiles to make as many patterns as possible. How many different patterns can he make?

a) 10.
b) 20.
c) 30.
d) 40.
e) 60.

5. I have chores to do around the house on a weekend. There are 5 chores I must complete by the end of the day. I can choose to do them in any order, so long as they are all completed. How many choices do I have?

a) 5.
b) 25.
c) 32.
d) 3125.
e) 120.

6. Next weekend, I have more chores to do around the house. There are 5 chores I must complete by the end of the day. I can choose to do any 2 of them in any order, and then do any 2 the next day again in any order, and then do the remaining 1 the following day. How many choices do I have?

a) 20.
b) 6.
c) 120.
d) 130.
e) 25.

7. A certain lottery play sheet has 10 numbers from which 5 have to be chosen. How many different ways can I pick the numbers?

a) 150.
b) 250.
c) 252.
d) 143.
e) 278.

8. At a buffet, there are 3 choices for an appetizer, 6 choices for a beverage, and 3 choices for an entrée. How many different ways can I select food from all the food choices?

a) 12.
b) 27.
c) 36.
d) 42.
e) 54.

9. If there is a basket of 10 assorted fruits, and I want to pick out 3 fruits, how many combinations of fruits do I have to choose from?

a) 130.
b) 210.
c) 310.
d) 120.
e) 100.

10. How many ways can I pick 3 numbers from a set of 10 numbers?

a) 720.
b) 120.
c) 180.
d) 150.
e) 880.

Test Your Knowledge: Fundamental Counting Principle, Permutations, Combinations – Answers

1. **c)**
   The number of ways = 4 * 3 * 5 * 2 * 3 = 360.

2. **b)**
   Multiply the possible number of choices for each item from which you can choose.

   2 * 3 * 2 * 2 = 24.

3. **c)**
   This is a combination problem. The order of the candidates does not matter.

   The number of combinations = 5!/3!(5 - 3)! = 5 * 4/2 * 1 = 10.

4. **e)**
   This is a permutation problem. The order in which the tiles are arranged is counted.

   The number of patterns = 5!/(5 - 3)! = 5 * 4 * 3 = 60.

5. **e)**
   This is a permutation problem. The order in which the chores are completed matters.

   ${}^{5}P_{5}$ = 5!/(5 - 5)! = 5! = 5 * 4 * 3 * 2 * 1 = 120.

6. **c)**
   $\#Choices_{today}$ = ${}^{5}P_{2}$ = 5!/(5 - 2)! = 5 * 4 = 20.

   $\#Choices_{tomorrow}$ = ${}^{3}P_{2}$ = 3!/1! = 6.

   $\#Choices_{day3}$ = 1.

   The total number of permutations = 20 * 6 * 1 = 120.

7. **c)**
   This is a combinations problem. The order of the numbers is not relevant.

   ${}^{10}n_{5}$ = 10!/5!(10 - 5)! = 10 * 9 * 8 * 7 * 6/5 * 4 * 3 * 2 * 1 = 252.

8. **e)**
   There are 3 ways to choose an appetizer, 6 ways to choose a beverage, and 3 ways to choose an entrée. The total number of choices = 3 * 6 * 3 = 54.

9. **d)**
   ${}^{10}C_{3}$ = 10!/(3!(10 - 3)!) = 10!/(3! * 7!) = 10 * 9 * 8/3 * 2 * 1 = 120.

10. **b)**
    ${}^{10}P_{4}$ = 10!/3!(10 - 3)! = 10 * 9 * 8/3 * 2 * 1 = 120

Test Your Knowledge: Ratios, Proportions, Rate of Change

1. A class has 50% more boys than girls. What is the ratio of boys to girls?
   a) 4:3.
   b) 3:2.
   c) 5:4.
   d) 10:7.
   e) 7:5.

2. A car can travel 30 miles on 4 gallons of gas. If the gas tank has a capacity of 16 gallons, how far can it travel if the tank is ¾ full?
   a) 120 miles.
   b) 90 miles.
   c) 60 miles.
   d) 55 miles.
   e) 65 miles.

3. The profits of a company increase by $5000 every year for five years and then decrease by $2000 for the next two years. What is the average rate of change in the company profit for that seven-year period?
   a) $1000/year.
   b) $2000/year.
   c) $3000/year.
   d) $4000/year.
   e) $5000/year.

4. A bag holds 250 marbles. Of those marbles, 40% are red, 30% are blue, 10% are green, and 20% are black. How many marbles of each color are present in the bag?
   a) Red = 90; Blue = 80; Green = 30; Black = 40.
   b) Red = 80; Blue = 60; Green = 30; Black = 80.
   c) Red = 100; Blue = 75; Green = 25; Black = 50.
   d) Red = 100; Blue = 70; Green = 30; Black = 50.
   e) Red = 120; Blue = 100; Green = 10; Black = 20.

5. Two students from a student body of 30 boys and 50 girls will be selected to serve on the school disciplinary committee. What is the probability that first a boy will be chosen, and then a girl?
   a) 1/1500.
   b) 1500/6400.
   c) 1500/6320.
   d) 1.
   e) 30/50.

6. If number *n*, divided by number *m*, gives a result of .5, what is the relationship between *n* and *m*?
   a) *n* is twice as big as *m*.
   b) *m* is three times as big as *n*.
   c) *n* is a negative number.
   d) *m* is a negative number.
   e) *n* is ½ of *m*.

7. In a fruit basket, there are 10 apples, 5 oranges, 5 pears, and 6 figs. If I select two fruits, what is the probability that I will first pick a pear and then an apple?
   a) .07.
   b) .08.
   c) 1/13.
   d) 13.
   e) 5.

8. In a fruit basket, there are 3 apples, 5 oranges, 2 pears, and 2 figs. If I pick out two fruits, what is the probability that I will pick a fig first and then an apple?
Round to the nearest 100th.
   a) .04.
   b) .05.
   c) .06.
   d) .03.
   e) .02.

9. If *x* workers can make p toys in *c* days, how many toys can y workers make in *d* days if they work at the same rate?
   a) *cp*/*qx*.
   b) *cq*/*px*.
   c) *cqy*/*px*.
   d) *pdy*/*cx*.
   e) *qy*/*px*.

10. If a car travels 35 miles on a gallon of gas, how far will it travel on 13 gallons of gas?
   a) 189 miles.
   b) 255 miles.
   c) 335 miles.
   d) 455 miles.
   e) 500 miles.

Test Your Knowledge: Ratios, Proportions, Rate of Change – Answers

1. **b)**
   The ratio of boys to girls is 150:100, or 3:2.

2. **b)**
   A full tank has 16 gallons → 3/4 of the tank = 12 gallons. The car can travel 30 miles on 4 gallons, so 12 gallons would take the car 12 * 30/4 = 90 miles.

3. **c)**
   Average Rate of Change = the change in value/change in time = (total profit – initial profit)/change in time. Initial profit = 0; change in time = 7 years.

   Increase = 5000 * 5 = 25000; decrease = 2000 * 2 = 4000; total profit = 25000 - 4000 = 21000.

   (21000 - 0)/7 years = $3000/year.

4. **c)**
   Total number of marbles = 250.

   #red marbles = 250 * 40/100 = 250 * .4 = 100.

   #blue marbles = 250 * .3 = 75.

   #green marbles = 250 * .1 = 25.

   #black marbles = 250 * .2 = 50.

5. **c)**
   The probability of selecting a boy from the entire group = 30:80.

   The probability of selecting a girl from the remaining group = 50:79.

   The probability of selecting a boy and a girl is (30:80) * (50:79) = 1500:6320.

6. **e)**
   If $n/m = .5$, then $n = .5m$, or $n = ½$ of m.

7. **c)**
   The total number of fruit = 26.

   The probability of picking a pear = 5:26.

   The probability of picking an apple = 10:25.

   The probability of picking a pear and an apple = 5:26 * 10:25 = 50:650 = 1:13.

8. b)
The total number of fruit = 12.

The probability of picking a fig = 2;12.

The probability of picking an apple = 3;11.

The probability of picking a fig and an apple = 2;12 * 3;11 = 6;132 = .045.

Round up to .05.

9. d)
The overall rate for x workers = the number of toys/ the number of days, *p/c*. The number of toys one worker makes per day (rate) = *p/cx*. If *q* is the number of toys *y* workers make, and the rates are equal, then the number of toys made = the rate *x*.

The number of days * the number of workers gives us *q* = *p/cx* (*dy*), so:

q = *pdy/cx*.

10. d)
The distance travelled = (35/1)(13) = 455 miles.

Chapter 2: Vocabulary and Grammar

It's time to review those basic techniques used to determine the meanings of words with which you are not familiar. Don't worry though! The good news is that you have been using various degrees of these techniques since you first began to speak.

We have not included a vocabulary list in this book, because reading definitions from a page is the worst way to improve word knowledge. Interaction, and seeing the words used in context, is the best way to learn. We recommend using flashcards to improve your vocabulary knowledge – there are many resources available online. The best we've found is www.vocabulary.com/il; but you should find what suits you specifically!

Below are techniques for improving and utilizing the vocabulary you already have.

Context Clues

The most fundamental vocabulary skill is using the context in which a word is used to determine its meaning. Your ability to observe sentences closely is extremely useful when it comes to understanding new vocabulary words.

There are two types of context that can help you understand the meaning of unfamiliar words: situational context and sentence context. Regardless of which context is present, these types of questions are not really testing your knowledge of vocabulary; rather, they test your ability to comprehend the meaning of a word through its usage.

Situational context is context that is presented by the setting or circumstances in which a word or phrase occurs. **Sentence context** occurs within the specific sentence that contains the vocabulary word. To figure out words using sentence context clues, you should first determine the most important words in the sentence.

There are four types of clues that can help you understand context, and therefore the meaning of a word:

- **Restatement** clues occur when the definition of the word is clearly stated in the sentence.

- **Positive/negative clues** can tell you whether a word has a positive or negative meaning.

- **Contrast clues** include the opposite meaning of a word. Words like *but*, *on the other hand*, and *however* are tip-offs that a sentence contains a contrast clue.

- **Specific detail clues** provide a precise detail that can help you understand the meaning of the word.

It is important to remember that more than one of these clues can be present in the same sentence. The more there are, the easier it will be to determine the meaning of the word. For example, the following sentence uses both restatement and positive/negative clues: *Janet suddenly found herself destitute, so poor she could barely afford to eat*. The second part of the sentence clearly indicates that *destitute* is a negative word. It also restates the meaning: very poor.

Example: I had a hard time reading her *illegible* handwriting.

a) neat
b) unsafe
c) sloppy
d) educated

Already, you know that this sentence is discussing something that is hard to read. Look at the word that *illegible* is describing: handwriting. Based on context clues, you can tell that *illegible* means that her handwriting is hard to read.
Next, look at the answer choices. Choice a), *neat,* is obviously a wrong answer because neat handwriting would not be difficult to read. Choices b) and d), *unsafe* and *educated,* don't make sense. Therefore, choice c), *sloppy,* is the best answer.

Example: The dog was *dauntless* in the face of danger, braving the fire to save the girl trapped inside the building.

a) difficult
b) fearless
c) imaginative
d) startled

Demonstrating bravery in the face of danger would be b) *fearless*. In this case, the restatement clue (*braving the fire*) tells you exactly what the word means.

Example: Beth did not spend any time preparing for the test, but Tyrone kept a *rigorous* study schedule.

a) strict
b) loose
c) boring
d) strange

In this case, the contrast word *but* tells us that Tyrone studied in a different way than Beth, which means it's a contrast clue. If Beth did not study hard, then Tyrone did. The best answer, therefore, is choice a).

Analyzing Words

As you no doubt know, determining the meaning of a word can be more complicated than just looking in a dictionary. A word might have more than one **denotation**, or definition; which one the author intends can only be judged by looking at the surrounding text. For example, the word *quack* can refer to the sound a duck makes, or to a person who publicly pretends to have a qualification which he or she does not actually possess.

A word may also have different **connotations**, which are the implied meanings and emotion a word evokes in the reader. For example, a cubicle is a simply a walled desk in an office, but for many the word implies a constrictive, uninspiring workplace. Connotations can vary greatly between cultures and even between individuals.

Lastly, authors might make use of **figurative language**, which is the use of a word to imply something other than the word's literal definition. This is often done by comparing two things. If you say *I felt like a* *butterfly when I got a new haircut*, the listener knows you don't resemble an insect but instead felt beautiful and transformed.

Nouns, Pronouns, Verbs, Adjectives, and Adverbs

Nouns

Nouns are people, places, or things. They are typically the subject of a sentence. For example, "The hospital was very clean." The noun is "hospital;" it is the "place."

Pronouns

Pronouns essentially "replace" nouns. This allows a sentence to not sound repetitive. Take the sentence: "Sam stayed home from school because Sam was not feeling well." The word "Sam" appears twice in the same sentence. Instead, you can use a pronoun and say, "Sam stayed at home because *he* did not feel well." Sounds much better, right?

Most Common Pronouns:

- I, me, mine, my.
- You, your, yours.
- He, him, his.
- She, her, hers.
- It, its.
- We, us, our, ours.
- They, them, their, theirs.

Verbs

Remember the old commercial, "Verb: It's what you do"? That sums up verbs in a nutshell! Verbs are the "action" of a sentence; verbs "do" things.

They can, however, be quite tricky. Depending on the subject of a sentence, the tense of the word (past, present, future, etc.), and whether or not they are regular or irregular, verbs have many variations.

Example: "He runs to second base." The verb is "runs." This is a "regular verb."

Example: "I am 7 years old." The verb in this case is "am." This is an "irregular verb."

As mentioned, verbs must use the correct tense – and that tense must remain the same throughout the sentence. "I was baking cookies and eat some dough." That sounded strange, didn't it? That's because the two verbs "baking" and "eat" are presented in different tenses. "Was baking" occurred in the past; "eat," on the other hand, occurs in the present. Instead, it should be "**ate** some dough."

Adjectives
Adjectives are words that describe a noun and give more information. Take the sentence: "The boy hit the ball." If you want to know more about the noun "boy," then you could use an adjective to describe it. "The **little** boy hit the ball." An adjective simply provides more information about a noun or subject in a sentence.

Adverbs
For some reason, many people have a difficult time with adverbs – but don't worry! They are really quite simple. Adverbs are similar to adjectives in that they provide more information; however, they describe verbs, adjectives, and even other adverbs. They do **not** describe nouns – that's an adjective's job.

Take the sentence: "The doctor said she hired a new employee."

It would give more information to say: "The doctor said she **recently** hired a new employee." Now we know more about *how* the action was executed. Adverbs typically describe when or how something has happened, how it looks, how it feels, etc.

Good vs. Well
A very common mistake that people make concerning adverbs is the misuse of the word "good."

"Good" is an adjective – things taste good, look good, and smell good. "Good" can even be a noun – "Superman does good" – when the word is speaking about "good" vs. "evil." HOWEVER, "good" is never an adverb.

People commonly say things like, "I did really good on that test," or, "I'm good." Ugh! This is NOT the correct way to speak! In those sentences, the word "good" is being used to describe an action: how a person **did**, or how a person **is**. Therefore, the adverb "well" should be used. "I did really **well** on that test." "I'm **well**."

The correct use of "well" and "good" can make or break a person's impression of your grammar – make sure to always speak correctly!

Study Tips for Improving Vocabulary and Grammar

1. You're probably pretty computer savvy and know the Internet very well. Visit the Online Writing Lab website, which is sponsored by Purdue University, at http://owl.english.purdue.edu. This site provides you with an excellent overview of syntax, writing style, and strategy. It also has helpful and lengthy review sections that include multiple-choice "Test Your Knowledge" quizzes, which provide immediate answers to the questions.

2. It's beneficial to read the entire passage first to determine its intended meaning BEFORE you attempt to answer any questions. Doing so provides you with key insight into a passage's syntax (especially verb tense, subject-verb agreement, modifier placement, writing style, and punctuation).

3. When you answer a question, use the "Process-of-Elimination Method" to determine the best answer. Try each of the four answers and determine which one BEST fits with the meaning of the paragraph. Find the BEST answer. Chances are that the BEST answer is the CORRECT answer.

Test Your Knowledge: Vocabulary and Grammar

1. "The medication must be properly administered to the patient."
   Which of the words in the above sentence is an adverb?
   a) Medication.
   b) Properly.
   c) Administered.
   d) Patient.

2. "The old man had trouble walking if he did not have his walker and had a long way to go."
   What is the subject of the sentence?
   a) Walker.
   b) His.
   c) Trouble.
   d) Man.

3. "The boy decided ___ would ride his bike now that the sun was shining."
   Which of the following pronouns completes the sentence?
   a) His.
   b) Him.
   c) He.
   d) They.

4. "The impatient student hurried through the test and failed as a result."
   Which word is an adjective?
   a) Hurried.
   b) Result.
   c) Impatient.
   d) Student.

5. Correct the verb: "The nurse decided it were a good time to follow up with a patient about their medication."
   a) Was.
   b) Is.
   c) Has.
   d) No error.

Use context clues to determine the meaning of each underlined word.

6. His story didn't seem very <u>realistic</u>; even though it was a documentary.
   a) Believable.
   b) Humorous.
   c) Poetic.
   d) Exciting.

7. Listening to music too loudly, especially through headphones, can impair your hearing.
  a) Damage.
  b) Heighten.
  c) Use.
  d) Ensure.

8. Kelly's game happened to coincide with the Sue's recital.
  a) Happen before.
  b) Occur at the same time.
  c) Occur afterward.
  d) Not happen.

9. The weather has been very extreme lately; thankfully, today it's much more temperate.
  a) Troubling.
  b) Beautiful.
  c) Cold.
  d) Moderate.

10. He knew he couldn't win the race after falling off his bike, so he had to concede.
  a) Continue.
  b) Give up.
  c) Challenge.
  d) Be thankful.

11. The editor, preferring a more terse writing style, cut 30% of the words from the article.
  a) Elegant.
  b) Factual.
  c) Descriptive.
  d) Concise.

12. Victor Frankenstein spent the last years of his life chasing his elusive monster, which was always one step ahead.
  a) Unable to be compared.
  b) Unable to be captured.
  c) Unable to be forgotten.
  d) Unable to be avoided.

13. Certain passages were taken from the book for the purpose of illustration.
  a) Excerpts.
  b) Contents.
  c) Paragraphs.
  d) Tables.

14. The investigator searched among the ruins for the cause of the fire.
  a) Terminal.
  b) Foundation.
  c) Rubble.
  d) Establishment.

15. To make her novels more engaging, Cynthia was known to embellish her writing with fictitious details.

a) Add to.
b) Detract.
c) Isolate.
d) Disavow.

16. Robert's well-timed joke served to diffuse the tension in the room and the party continued happily.

a) Refuse.
b) Intensify.
c) Create.
d) Soften.

17. I had a difficult time understanding the book because the author kept digressing to unrelated topics.

a) Deviating, straying.
b) Regressing, reverting.
c) Changing the tone.
d) Expressing concisely.

18. The senator evaded almost every question.

a) Avoided.
b) Answered indirectly.
c) Refused to answer directly.
d) Deceived.

19. Sammie hasn't come out of her room all afternoon, but I would surmise that it is because she is upset about not being able to go to the mall.

a) Confirm.
b) Surprise.
c) Believe.
d) Guess.

20. The details can be worked out later; what's important is that the company follows the crux of the argument, which is that everyone be paid equally.

a) Overall tone.
b) Specific fact.
c) Main point.
d) Logic, reasoning.

Use context clues to choose the best word to complete the sentence.

21. Mr. Collins ______ tomatoes so vehemently that he felt ill just smelling them.

a) Resented
b) Disliked
c) Detested
d) Hated

22. We were rolling on the ground with laughter during the ______ new movie.

a) Comical
b) Humorous
c) Amusing
d) Hilarious

23. Tina's parents made us feel right at home during our visit to their house with their generous _______.

a) Unselfishness
b) Politeness
c) Hospitality
d) Charity

24. Although his mother was not happy that he broke the window, she was pleased that he was _____ about it.

a) Honest
b) Trustworthy
c) Authentic
d) Decent

25. The soldiers ______ to their feet immediately when then officer walked into the room.

a) Stood
b) Leapt
c) Rose
d) Skipped

Test Your Knowledge: Vocabulary and Grammar – Answers

1. **b)**
   "Properly" is the adverb which describes the verb "administered."

2. **d)**
   Although there are other nouns in the sentence, the "man" is the subject.

3. **c)**
   "He" is the correct answer; the other pronouns are possessive or otherwise in the wrong tense.

4. **c)**
   "Impatient" describes the noun "student."

5. **a)**
   "Was" is the correct answer; the other choices are in the wrong tense.

6. a) **Believable**.
   Realistic means accurate, truthful, and believable.

7. a) **Damage.**
   This is the only logical choice.

8. b) **Occur at the same time**.
   According to information in the sentence, the game was scheduled at the same time as the recital.

9. d) **Moderate**.
   The context says that the weather has been "extreme." It does not say if the weather has been extremely hot or cold; therefore, choices **b) Beautiful** and **c) Cold** can be ruled out. The sentence also indicates a change from negative to positive making moderate the best choice.

10. b) **Give up**.
    The speaker of the sentence knows they cannot win, so choice **b)** is the best choice.

11. d) **Concise.**
    Terse means concise, using no unnecessary words. The main clue is that the editor cut words from the article, reducing its wordiness.

12. b) **Unable to be captured.**
    Elusive means evasive, difficult to capture.

13. a) **Excerpt.**
    An excerpt is a passage or quote from a book, article, or other publication

14. c) **Rubble** is synonymous with ruin.

15. a) **Add to**.
    To embellish is to add details to a story to make it more appealing.

16. d) Softën.

The clues *tension* and *continue happily* tell you that **d)** is the best choice

17. a) To deviate, stray.

To digress means to deviate; to stray from the main subject in writing or speaking.

18. a) To avoid.

To evade means to avoid by cleverness. The senator avoids answering the question by changing the subject.

19. d) Guess.

The speaker is guessing why Samantha is upset based on circumstances; she has not actually given a reason.

20. c) Main point.

Crux means the central or main point, especially of a problem. The main context clue is that the speaker isn't concerned with the details but is focused on getting agreement on the main point.

21. c) Detested.

The knowledge that Mr. Collins feels ill just smelling tomatoes suggests that his hatred for tomatoes is intense; therefore, the best choice will be the most negative. To **dislike** tomatoes – choice **b)** – is the most neutral word, so this choice can be ruled out. **Resented** is a word that generally applies to people or their actions, ruling out choice **a).** Given the choice between **c)** and **d),** the most negative is **c) Detested.**

22. d) Hilarious.

The movie must be extremely funny for the audience to have this sort of reaction, and, while all of the answer choices are synonyms for funny, the only one that means extremely funny is choice **d) Hilarious.**

23. c) Hospitality.

Although all four choices describe different types of kindness, **unselfishness** – choice **a)** – can be ruled out because it has the same basic meaning as the adjective, generous. Choice **d) Charity** is a kindness usually associated with those less fortunate; since nothing in the context indicates this type of relationship, this choice can also be eliminated.

Left with choices **b) Politeness** and **c) Hospitality**, hospitality best describes the kindness of welcoming someone into your home.

24. a) Honest.

Again we have a case in which all of the word choices are synonyms for the word honest. In this case, the most neutral word is the best choice. Choice **b) Trustworthy**, **c) Authentic**, and **d) Decent** do not make as much sense as the most basic synonym, **honest.**

25. b) Leapt. The word immediately is the main clue. **a) Stood** and **c) Rose** are neutral words that do not convey a sense of urgency. Choice **b) Leapt** is the only word that implies the immediacy demanded by the sentence context.

Chapter 3: Spelling and Word Knowledge

Word Structure

Although you are not expected to know every word in the English language for your test, you will need the ability to use deductive reasoning to find the choice that is the best match for the word in question, which is why we are going to explain how to break a word into its parts to determine its meaning. Many words can be broken down into three main parts:

prefix – root – suffix

Roots are the building blocks of all words. Every word is either a root itself or has a root. Just as a plant cannot grow without roots, neither can vocabulary, because a word must have a root to give it meaning. The root is what is left when you strip away all the prefixes and suffixes from a word. For example, in the word *unclear*, if you take away the prefix *un-*, you have the root *clear*.

Roots are not always recognizable words, because they generally come from Latin or Greek words, such as *nat*, a Latin root meaning born. The word *native*, which means a person born in a referenced placed, comes from this root, so does the word *prenatal*, meaning beforc birth. It's important to keep in mind, however, that roots do not always match the exact definitions of words, and they can have several different spellings.

Prefixes are syllables added to the beginning of a word and **suffixes** are syllables added to the end of the word. Both carry assigned meanings and can be attached to a word to completely change the word's meaning or to enhance the word's original meaning.

Let's use the word prefix itself as an example: *fix* means to place something securely and *pre-* means before. Therefore, *prefix* means to place something before or in front. Now let's look at a suffix: in the word *feminism*, *femin* is a root which means female. The suffix *-ism* means act, practice, or process. Thus, *feminism* is the process of establishing equal rights for women.

Although you cannot determine the meaning of a word by a prefix or suffix alone, you can use this knowledge to eliminate answer choices; understanding whether the word is positive or negative can give you the partial meaning of the word.

Test Your Knowledge: Spelling and Word Knowledge

Try to find the root in each of the underlined words.

1. The bridge was out, so the river was impassable.
   a) Im-
   b) -pass-
   c) -a-
   d) -able

2. I am usually on time, but my husband is chronically late.
   a) Chron-
   b) -chronical-
   c) -ally-
   d) -ic

3. The only way to succeed is by striving to do your best.
   a) Str-
   a) Striv-
   b) Strive-
   c) -ing

4. We drifted along lazily on the tranquil river.
   a) Tra-
   b) -qui-
   c) Tranq-
   d) -uil

5. A pediatrician is a doctor who takes care of children.
   a) Ped-
   b) -ia-
   c) -tri-
   d) -cian

Choose the word that shares the same root as the given word.

6. Audible:
   a) Auditorium.
   b) Because.
   c) Dribble.
   d) Bagel.

7. Nominate:
   a) Eaten.
   b) Minute.
   c) Hated.
   d) Synonym.

8. Disappoint:

a) Disappear.
b) Appointment.
c) Interest.
d) Potato.

9. Dilute:

a) Flute.
b) Dictate.
c) Pollute.
d) Hesitate.

10. Sympathy:

a) System.
b) Empathy.
c) Pattern.
d) Rhythm.

11. Science:

a) Conscious.
b) Once.
c) Alien.
d) Parasite.

12. Incline:

a) Recline.
b) Independent.
c) Cluster.
d) Twine.

For each question below, use the Latin root to determine the meaning of the underlined word.

13. An <u>amiable</u> person is:

a) Talkative, loud.
b) Truthful, honest.
c) Highly educated.
d) Friendly, good-natured.

14. A <u>lucid</u> argument:

a) Is very clear and intelligible.
b) Is loosely held together, tenuous.
c) Frequently digresses.
d) Errs repeatedly in its logic.

15. A <u>complacent</u> person:

a) Frequently makes mistakes, but does not accept responsibility.
b) Likes to pick fights.
c) Is contented to a fault, self-satisfied.
d) Is known to tell lies, embellish the truth.

16. To exacerbate a problem means:
a) To solve it.
b) To analyze it.
c) To lessen it.
d) To worsen it.

17. To measure the veracity of something is to measure its:
a) Value or worth.
b) Truthfulness.
c) Weight.
d) Life force.

18. Something that is eloquent is:
a) Dull, trite, hackneyed.
b) Expressed in a powerful and effective manner.
c) Very old, antiquated.
d) Equally divided or apportioned.

19. To indict someone is to:
a) Pick a fight with that person.
b) Stop or block that person from doing something.
c) Charge that person with a crime.
d) Love that person dearly.

20. A quiescent place is:
a) Very isolated.
b) Tumultuous, chaotic.
c) Sacred.
d) Still, at rest.

What are the affixes in each word?

21. Disease:
a) Dis-.
b) -ise-.
c) -eas-.
d) -ase.

22. Uncomfortable:
a) Un-.
b) Un-, -com-.
c) -fort-.
d) Un-, -able.

23. Disrespected:
a) Re-, -spect, -ed.
b) Dis-, -ed.
c) Dis-, re-, -ed.
d) Respect-, -ed.

24. Impressive:

a) Im-, -ive.
b) -ive.
c) Press-, -ive.
d) Impre-, -ive.

25. Predated:

a) Pre-.
b) Pre-, -d.
c) Pre-, -ed.
d) –d.

Using your knowledge of prefixes and root words, try to determine the meaning of the words in the following questions.

26. To take <u>precaution</u> is to:

a) Prepare before doing something.
b) Remember something that happened earlier.
c) Become aware of something for the first time.
d) Try to do something again.

27. To <u>reorder</u> a list is to:

a) Use the same order again.
b) Put the list in a new order.
c) Get rid of the list.
d) Find the list.

28. An <u>antidote</u> to a disease is:

a) Something that is part of the disease.
b) Something that works against the disease.
c) Something that makes the disease worse.
d) Something that has nothing to do with the disease.

29. Someone who is <u>multiethnic:</u>

a) Likes only certain kinds of people.
b) Lives in the land of his or her birth.
c) Is from a different country.
d) Has many different ethnicities.

30. Someone who is <u>misinformed</u> has been:

a) Taught something new.
b) Told the truth.
c) Forgotten.
d) Given incorrect information.

Choose the best answer to each question. (Remember you are looking for the closest meaning.)

31. Exorbitant means:

a) Belonging to a group.
b) To orbit.
c) Beneath conscious awareness.
d) Far beyond what is normal or reasonable.

32. Denunciation means:

a) To denounce or openly condemn.
b) Critical, of or like a condemnation.
c) One who denounces or openly condemns another.
d) The act of denouncing or openly condemning.

33. Metamorphosis means:

a) To transform.
b) One who has changed.
c) A transformation.
d) Tending to change frequently.

34. To reconcile means:

a) To reestablish a close relationship between.
b) To move away from.
c) To undermine.
d) To surpass or outdo.

35. Didactic means:

a) A teacher or instructor.
b) Intended to instruct, moralizing.
c) To preach or moralize.
d) The process of instructing.

36. Unilateral means:

a) To multiply.
b) Understated.
c) Literal.
d) One-sided.

37. Subordinate means:

a) Under someone else's authority or control.
b) Organized according to rank; hierarchical.
c) Something ordinary or average, without distinction.
d) Repeated frequently to aid memorization.

38. Incisive means:

a) Insight.
b) Worthy of consideration.
c) Penetrating.
d) To act forcefully.

39. Intermittent means:

a) Badly handled.
b) Occurring at intervals
c) Greatly varied.
d) A number between one and ten.

40. Miscreant means:

a) Someone who is unconventional.
b) Someone who lacks creativity.
c) A very naive person.
d) An evil person or villain.

Test Your Knowledge: Spelling and Word Knowledge – Answers

1. **b) –pass-** .

2. **a) Chron-**.

3. **c) Strive-**.

4. **b) –qui-**.
   Quies is a Latin root meaning rest or quiet.

5. **a) Ped-**.
   Ped is a Latin root meaning child or education. You might recognize that the suffix **-cian** refers to what someone does, such as physician or beautician. The suffix **-iatr** relates to doctors, as you can see in the words psychiatry and podiatry. Both suffixes support the root of the word.

6. **a) Auditorium**.
   From the Latin root **aud**, meaning hearing or listening.

7. **d) Synonym**.
   The words nominate and synonym share the root, **nom**, meaning name. Remember, roots are not necessarily going to be in the same position in other words.

8. **b) Appointment**.
   Greek root **poie**, meaning to make.

9. **c) Pollute**.
   Both dilute and pollute come from the root **lut**, meaning to wash.

10. **b) Empathy**.
    The words sympathy and empathy come from the Greek root **path,** meaning feeling, suffering, or disease.

11. **a) Conscious**.
    Science and conscious share the Latin root **sci,** which means to know.

12. **a) Recline**.
    The words incline and recline both share the Greek root ***clin*****,** meaning to lean toward or bend.

13. **d)**
    The root **am** means love. Amiable means friendly and agreeable or good natured, likeable, or pleasing.

14. **a)**
    The root **luc/lum/lus** means light. Lucid means very clear, easy to understand, intelligible.

15. **c)**
    The root **plac** means to please. Complacent means contented to a fault; self-satisfied (pleased with oneself).

16. d) The root **ac** means sharp, bitter. To exacerbate means to make worse or to increase the severity, violence, or bitterness of.

17. b)
The root **ver** means truth. Veracity means truth or truthfulness.

18. b)
The root **loc/log/loqu** means word or speech. Eloquent means expressed in a powerful, fluent, and persuasive manner.

19. c)
The root **dic/dict/dit** means to say, tell, or use words. To indict means to formally accuse of or charge with a crime.

20. d)
The root **qui** means quiet. Quiescent means inactive, quiet, or at rest.

21. a) Dis-.
The prefix **dis-** means away from, deprive of, reversal, or not. If someone has a **disease** they are not well.

22. d) Un-, **-able**.
The prefix **un-** means not. The suffix **-able** means ability or worthy of. **Uncomfortable** means not able to be in a state of comfort.

23. c) Dis-, **re-**, **-ed**.
The prefix **dis-** means away from, reversal, or not. The prefix **re-** means back or again. The suffix **-ed** indicates that the word is in the past tense. **Disrespected** means showed a lack of respect towards.

24. a) Im-, **-ive**.
The prefix **im-** means in, into, or within. The suffix **-ive** means having the nature of. **Impressive** means having the ability inspire an internal feeling of awe.

25. c) Pre-, **-ed**.
The prefix **pre-** means before. The suffix **-ed** indicates that the word is in the past tense. **Predated** means came before the date.

26. a) Prepare before doing something.
Pre- means before; to take **caution** is to be careful or take heed.

27. b) Put the list in a new order.
Re- means again. In this case, order means organize. Reorder then means to organize the list again or to put the list into a different order.

28. b) Something that works against the disease.
The prefix **anti-** means against. An **antidote** is something that works against a disease or a poison.

29. d) Has many different ethnicities.
The prefix **multi-** means many. Someone who is **multiethnic** has relatives from many different ethnic groups.

30. d) Given incorrect information.
Mis- means opposite, and to be **informed** is to have the correct information.

31. d) Far beyond what is normal or reasonable.
The prefix **ex-** means out, out of, away from.

32. a) The act of denouncing or openly condemning.
The prefix **de-** means against, the root **nounc** means to state or declare, and the noun suffix **-tion** means the act or state of.

33. c) A transformation.
The prefix **meta-** means change, while the root **morph** means shape or form, and the **noun** suffix **-sis** means the process of. **Metamorphosis** means a marked change of form or a transformation.

34. a) Means to reestablish a relationship.
The prefix **re-** means back or again and, the root **con** means with. Together they mean back together again or reestablishing a relationship.

35. b) Intended to instruct or moralize.
The adjective suffix **-ic** means pertaining or relating to, having the quality of. Only choices **b)** and **d)** define a quality, and choice **d)** would require an additional suffix.

36. d) One-sided.
The prefix **uni-** means one.

37. a) Under someone else's authority or control.
The prefix **sub-** means under, beneath or below.

38. c) Penetrating.
The adjective suffix **-ive** means having the nature of.

39. b) Occurring at intervals.
The prefix **inter-** means between or among.

40. d) An evil person or villain.
The prefix **mis-** means bad, evil, or wrong. The suffix **–ant** means an agent or something that performs the action.

Chapter 4: Reading

The Reading section measures your ability to understand, analyze, and evaluate written passages. The passages will contain material from a variety of sources, and will cover a number of different topics.

Strategies

Despite the different types of questions you will face, there are some strategies for Reading Comprehension which apply across the board:

- Read the answer choices first, then read the passage. This will save you time, as you will know what to look out for as you read.

- Use the process of elimination. Some answer choices are obviously incorrect and are relatively easy to detect. After reading the passage, eliminate those blatantly incorrect answer choices; this increases your chance of finding the correct answer much more quickly.

- Avoid negative statements. Generally, test-makers will not make negative statements about anyone or anything. Statements will be either neutral or positive, so if it seems like an answer choice has a negative connotation, it is very likely that the answer is intentionally false.

The Main Idea

The main idea of a text is the purpose behind why a writer would choose to write a book, article, story, etc. Being able to find and understand the main idea is a critical skill necessary to comprehend and appreciate what you're reading.

Imagine that you're at a friend's home for the evening.
He says, "Hey, I think we should watch this movie tonight. Is that ok with you?"
"Yeah, that sounds good," you reply. "What's it about?"

You'd like to know a little about what you'll be watching, but your question may not get you a satisfactory answer, because you've only asked about the topic of the film. The **topic**—what the movie is about—is only half the story. Think, for example, about all the alien invasion films ever been made.

While these films may share the same general subject, what they have to say about the aliens or about humanity's theoretical response to invasion may be very different. Each filmmaker has different ideas or opinions she wants to convey about a topic, just as writers write because they have something to say about a particular topic. When you look beyond the facts to the argument the writer is making about his topic, you're looking for the **main idea**.

One more quick note: the PSB may also ask about a passage's **theme**, which is similar to but distinct from its topic. While a topic is usually a specific *person, place, thing*, or *issue,* the theme is an *idea* or *concept* that the author refers back to frequently. Examples of common themes include ideas like the importance of family, the dangers of technology, and the beauty of nature.
There will be many questions on the PSB that require you to differentiate between the topic, theme, and main idea of a passage. Let's look at an example passage to see how you would answer these questions.

Example: "Babe Didrikson Zaharias, one of the most decorated female athletes of the twentieth century, is an inspiration for everyone. Born in 1911 in Beaumont, Texas, Zaharias lived in a time when women were considered second-class to men, but she never let that stop her from becoming a champion. Babe was one of seven children in a poor immigrant family, and was competitive from an early age. As a child she excelled at most things she tried, especially sports, which continued into high school and beyond. After high school, Babe played amateur basketball for two years, and soon after began training in track and field. Despite the fact that women were only allowed to enter in three events, Babe represented the United States in the 1932 Los Angeles Olympics, and won two gold medals and one silver for track and field events.

"In the early 1930s, Babe began playing golf which earned her a legacy. The first tournament she entered was a men's only tournament, however she did not make the cut to play. Playing golf as an amateur was the only option for a woman at this time, since there was no professional women's league. Babe played as an amateur for a little over a decade, until she turned pro in 1947 for the Ladies Professional Golf Association (LPGA) of which she was a founding member. During her career as a golfer, Babe won eighty-two tournaments, amateur and professional, including the U.S. Women's Open, All-American Open, and British Women's Open Golf Tournament. In 1953, Babe was diagnosed with cancer, but fourteen weeks later, she played in a tournament. That year she won her third U.S. Women's Open. However by 1955, she didn't have the physicality to compete anymore, and she died of the disease in 1956."

The topic of this paragraph is obviously Babe Zaharias—the whole passage describes events from her life. But what is the main idea of this paragraph? You might be tempted to answer, *Babe Zaharias*, or *Babe Zaharias' life*. Yes, Babe Zaharias' life is the topic of the passage—who or what the passage is about—but the topic is not the main idea. The main idea is what the writer wants to say about this subject. What is the writer saying about Babe Zaharias' life? She's saying that she's someone to admire—that's the main idea and what unites all the information in the paragraph. Lastly, what might the theme of the passage be? The writer refers to several broad concepts, including never giving up and overcoming the odds, both of which could be themes for the passage.

The example above shows two important characteristics of a main idea:

- It is general enough to encompass all of the ideas in the passage. The main idea of a passage should be broad enough for all of the other sentences in that passage to fit underneath it, like people under an umbrella.

- It asserts a specific viewpoint that the author supports with facts, opinions, or other details. In other words, the main idea takes a stand.

Example: "From so far away it's easy to imagine the surface of our solar system's planets as enigmas—how could we ever know what those far-flung planets really look like? It turns out, however, that scientists have a number of tools at their disposal that allow them to paint detailed pictures of many planets' surfaces. The topography of Venus, for example, has been explored by several space probes, including the Russian Venera landers and NASA's Magellan orbiter. These craft used imaging and radar to map the surface of the planet, identifying a whole host of features including volcanoes, craters, and a complex system of channels. Mars has similarly been mapped by space probes, including the famous Mars Rovers, which are automated vehicles that actually landed on the surface of Mars. These rovers have been used by NASA and other space agencies to study the geology, climate, and possible biology of the planet.

"In addition these long-range probes, NASA has also used its series of orbiting telescopes to study distant planets. These four massively powerful telescopes include the famous Hubble Space Telescope as well as the Compton Gamma Ray Observatory, Chandra X-Ray Observatory, and the Spitzer Space Telescope. Scientists can use these telescopes to examine planets using not only visible light but also infrared and near-infrared light, ultraviolet light, x-rays and gamma rays.

"Powerful telescopes aren't just found in space: NASA makes use of Earth-bound telescopes as well. Scientists at the National Radio Astronomy Observatory in Charlottesville, VA, have spent decades using radio imaging to build an incredibly detailed portrait of Venus' surface. In fact, Earth-bound telescopes offer a distinct advantage over orbiting telescopes because they allow scientists to capture data from a fixed point, which in turn allows them to effectively compare data collected over long period of time."

Which of the following sentences best describes the main of the passage?

a) It's impossible to know what the surfaces of other planets are really like.
b) Telescopes are an important tool for scientists studying planets in our solar system.
c) Venus' surface has many of the same features as the Earth's, including volcanoes, craters, and channels.
d) Scientists use a variety of advanced technologies to study the surface of the planets in our solar system.

Answer a) can be eliminated because it directly contradicts the rest of the passage, which goes into detail about how scientists have learned about the surfaces of other planets. Answers b) and c) can also be eliminated because they offer only specific details from the passage—while both choices contain details from the passage, neither is general enough to encompass the passage as a whole. Only answer d) provides an assertion that is both backed up by the passage's content and general enough to cover the entire passage.

Topic and Summary Sentences

Writers sometimes lead with preliminary sentences that give the reader clear ideas of what the text is about. A sentence that encompasses the main idea of the text is the topic sentence.
Notice, for example, how the first sentence in the example paragraph about Babe Zaharias states the main idea: *Babe Didrikson Zaharias, one of the most decorated female athletes of the twentieth century, is an inspiration for everyone.*

Topic sentences are often found at the beginning of paragraphs. Sometimes, though, writers begin with specific supporting details and lead up to the main idea; in this case the topic sentence is found at the end of the paragraph. In other cases there isn't a clear topic sentence at all—but that doesn't mean there isn't a main idea; the author has just chosen not to express it in a clear topic sentence. You may also see a **summary sentence** at the end of a passage. As its name suggests, this sentence sums up the passage, often by restating the main idea and the author's key evidence supporting it.

Example: In the following paragraph, what are the topic and summary sentences?

"The Constitution of the United States establishes a series of limits to rein in centralized power. Separation of powers distributes federal authority among three competing branches: the executive, the legislative, and the judicial. Checks and balances allow the branches to check the usurpation of power by any one branch. States' rights are protected under the Constitution from too much encroachment by the federal government. Enumeration of powers names the specific and few powers the federal government has. These four restrictions have helped sustain the American republic for over two centuries."

The topic sentence is the first sentence in the paragraph. It introduces the topic of discussion, in this case the constitutional limits aimed at resisting centralized power. The summary sentence is the last sentence in the paragraph. It sums up the information that was just presented: here, that constitutional limits have helped sustain the United States of America for over two hundred years.

Implied Main Idea

When there's no clear topic sentence, you're looking for an **implied main idea**. This requires some detective work: you will need to look at the author's word choice and tone in addition to the content of the passage to find his or her main idea. Let's look at an example paragraph.

Example: "One of my summer reading books was *Mockingjay*. Though it's several hundred pages long, I read it in just a few days. I couldn't wait to see what happened to Katniss, the main character. But by the time I got to the end, I wondered if I should have spent my week doing something else. The ending was such a letdown that I completely forgot that I'd enjoyed most of the book."

There's no topic sentence here, but you should still be able to find the main idea. Look carefully at what the writer says and how she says it. What is she suggesting?

a) *Mockingjay* is a terrific novel.
b) *Mockingjay* is disappointing.
c) *Mockingjay* is full of suspense.
d) *Mockingjay* is a lousy novel.

The correct answer is b): the novel is disappointing. How can you tell that this is the main idea? First, you can eliminate choice c) because it's too specific to be a main idea. It only deals with one specific aspect of the novel (its suspense). Sentences a), b), and d), on the other hand, all express a larger idea about the quality of the novel. However, only one of these statements can actually serve as a "net" for the whole paragraph. Notice that while the first few sentences praise the novel, the last two criticize it. Clearly, this is a mixed review.
Therefore, the best answer is b). Sentence a) is too positive and doesn't account for the "letdown" of an ending. Sentence d), on the other hand, is too negative and doesn't account for the reader's sense of suspense and interest in the main character. But sentence b) allows for both positive and negative aspects—when a good thing turns bad, we often feel disappointed.

Example: "Fortunately, none of Alyssa's coworkers has ever seen inside the large filing drawer in her desk. Disguised by the meticulous neatness of the rest of her workspace, there was no sign of the chaos beneath. To even open it, she had to struggle for several minutes with the enormous pile of junk jamming the drawer, until it would suddenly give way, and papers, folders, and candy wrappers spilled out of the top and onto the floor. It was an organizational nightmare, with torn notes and spreadsheets haphazardly thrown on top of each other, and melted candy smeared across pages. She was worried the odor would soon permeate to her coworker's desks, revealing to them her secret."

Which of the following expresses the main idea of this paragraph?

a) Alyssa wishes she could move to a new desk.
b) Alyssa wishes she had her own office.
c) Alyssa is glad none of her coworkers know about her messy drawer.
d) Alyssa is sad because she doesn't have any coworkers.

What the paragraph adds up to is that Alyssa is terribly embarrassed about her messy drawer, and she's glad that none of her coworkers have seen it, making C) the correct answer choice. This is the main idea. The paragraph opens with the word "fortunately," so we know that she thinks it's a good thing that none of her coworkers have seen inside the drawer. Plus, notice how the drawer is described: "it was an organizational nightmare," and it apparently doesn't even function properly – "to even open the drawer, she had to struggle for several minutes…" The writer reveals that it has an odor, with "melted candy" inside. Alyssa is clearly ashamed of her drawer and worries about what her coworkers would think if they saw inside it.

Supporting Details

Supporting details provide more support for the author's main idea. For instance, in the Babe Zaharias example above, the writer makes the general assertion that *Babe Didrikson Zaharias, one of the most decorated female athletes of the twentieth century, is an inspiration for everyone*. The other sentences offer specific facts and details that prove why Babe Zaharias is an inspiration: the struggles she faced as a female athlete, and the specific years she competed in the Olympics and in golf.

Writers often provide clues that can help you identify supporting details. These **signal words** tell you that a supporting fact or idea will follow, and so can be helpful in identifying supporting details. Signal words can also help you rule out sentences that are not the main idea or topic sentence: if a sentence begins with one of these phrases, it will likely be too specific to be a main idea.

Questions on the PSB will ask you to do two things with supporting details: you will need to find details that support a particular idea and also explain why a particular detail was included in the passage. In order to answer these questions, you need to have a solid understanding of the passage's main idea. With this knowledge, you can determine how a supporting detail fits in with the larger structure of the passage.

Example: "From so far away it's easy to imagine the surface of our solar system's planets as enigmas—how could we ever know what those far-flung planets really look like? It turns out, however, that scientists have a number of tools at their disposal that allow them to paint detailed pictures of many planets' surfaces. The topography of Venus, for example, has been explored by several space probes, including the Russian *Venera* landers and NASA's *Magellan* orbiter. These craft used imaging and radar to map the surface of the planet, identifying a whole host of features including volcanoes, craters, and a complex system of channels. Mars has similarly been mapped by space probes, including the famous Mars Rovers, which are automated vehicles that actually landed on the surface of Mars. These rovers have been used by NASA and other space agencies to study the geology, climate, and possible biology of the planet.

"In addition these long-range probes, NASA has also used its series of orbiting telescopes to study distant planets. These four massively powerful telescopes include the famous Hubble Space Telescope as well as the Compton Gamma Ray Observatory, Chandra X-Ray Observatory, and the Spitzer Space Telescope. Scientists can use these telescopes to examine planets using not only visible light but also infrared and near-infrared light, ultraviolet light, x-rays and gamma rays.

"Powerful telescopes aren't just found in space: NASA makes use of Earth-bound telescopes as well. Scientists at the National Radio Astronomy Observatory in Charlottesville, VA, have spent decades using radio imaging to build an incredibly detailed portrait of Venus' surface. In fact, Earth-bound telescopes offer a distinct advantage over orbiting telescopes because they allow scientists to capture data from a fixed point, which in turn allows them to effectively compare data collected over long period of time."

Which sentence from the text best helps develop the idea that scientists make use of many different technologies to study the surfaces of other planets?

a) These rovers have been used by NASA and other space agencies to study the geology, climate, and possible biology of the planet.
b) From so far away it's easy to imagine the surface of our solar system's planets as enigmas—how could we ever know what those far-flung planets really look like?
c) In addition these long-range probes, NASA has also used its series of orbiting telescopes to study distant planets.
d) These craft used imaging and radar to map the surface of the planet, identifying a whole host of features including volcanoes, craters, and a complex system of channels.

You're looking for detail from the passage that supports the main idea—scientists make use of many different technologies to study the surfaces of other planets. Answer a) includes a specific detail about rovers, but does not offer any details that support the idea of multiple technologies being used. Similarly, answer d) provides another specific detail about space probes. Answer b) doesn't provide any supporting details; it simply introduces the topic of the passage. Only answer c) provides a detail that directly supports the author's assertion that scientists use multiple technologies to study the planets.

If true, which detail could be added to the passage above to support the author's argument that scientists use many different technologies to study the surface of planets?

a) Because the Earth's atmosphere blocks x-rays, gamma rays, and infrared radiation, NASA needed to put telescopes in orbit above the atmosphere.
b) In 2015, NASA released a map of Venus which was created by compiling images from orbiting telescopes and long-range space probes.
c) NASA is currently using the *Curiosity* and *Opportunity* rovers to look for signs of ancient life on Mars.
d) NASA has spent over $2.5 billion to build, launch, and repair the Hubble Space Telescope.

You can eliminate answers c) and d) because they don't address the topic of studying the surface of planets. Answer a) can also be eliminated because it only addresses a single technology. Only choice b) provides would add support to the author's claim about the importance of using multiple technologies.

The author likely included the detail *Earth-bound telescopes offer a distinct advantage over orbiting telescopes because they allow scientists to capture data from a fixed point* in order to:

a) Explain why it has taken scientists so long to map the surface of Venus.
b) Suggest that Earth-bound telescopes are the most important equipment used by NASA scientists.
c) Prove that orbiting telescopes will soon be replaced by Earth-bound telescopes.
d) Demonstrate why NASA scientists rely on my different types of scientific equipment.

Only answer d) directs directly to the author's main argument. The author doesn't mention how long it has taken to map the surface of Venus (answer a), nor does he say that one technology is more important than the others (answer b). And while this detail does highlight the advantages of using Earth-bound telescopes, the author's argument is that many technologies are being used at the same time, so there's no reason to think that orbiting telescopes will be replaced (answer c).

Text Structure

Authors can structure passages in a number of different ways. These distinct organizational patterns, referred to as **text structure**, use the logical relationships between ideas to improve the readability and coherence of a text. The most common ways passages are organized include:

- **problem-solution**: the author presents a problem and then discusses a solution
- **comparison-contrast**: the author presents two situations and then discusses the similarities and differences
- **cause-effect**: the author presents an action and then discusses the resulting effects
- **descriptive**: an idea, object, person, or other item is described in detail

Example: "The issue of public transportation has begun to haunt the fast-growing cities of the southern United States. Unlike their northern counterparts, cities like Atlanta, Dallas, and Houston have long promoted growth out and not up—these are cities full of sprawling suburbs and single-family homes, not densely concentrated skyscrapers and apartments. What to do then, when all those suburbanites need to get into the central business districts for work? For a long time it seemed highways were the answer: twenty-lane wide expanses of concrete that would allow commuters to move from home to work and back again. But these modern miracles have become time-sucking, pollution spewing nightmares. They may not like it, but it's time for these cities to turn toward public transport like trains and buses if they want their cities to remain livable."

The organization of this passage can best be described as:

a) a comparison of two similar ideas
b) a description of a place
c) a discussion of several effects all related to the same cause
d) a discussion of a problem followed by the suggestion of a solution

You can exclude answer choice c) because the author provides no root cause or a list of effects. From there this question gets tricky, because the passage contains structures similar to those described above. For example, it compares two things (cities in the North and South) and describes a place (a sprawling city). However, if you look at the overall organization of the passage, you can see that it starts by presenting a problem (transportation) and then presents a solution (trains and buses), making answer d) the only choice that encompasses the entire passage.

The Author's Purpose

Whenever an author writes a text, she always has a purpose, whether that's to entertain, inform, explain, or persuade. A short story, for example, is meant to entertain, while an online news article would be designed to inform the public about a current event.

Each of these different types of writing has a specific name. On the PSB, you will be asked to identify which of these categories a passage fits into:

- **Narrative writing** tells a story. (novel, short story, play)
- **Expository writing** informs people. (newspaper and magazine articles)
- **Technical writing** explains something. (product manual, directions)
- **Persuasive writing** tries to convince the reader of something. (opinion column on a blog)

You may also be asked about primary and secondary sources. These terms describe not the writing itself but the author's relationship to what's being written about. A **primary source** is an unaltered piece of writing that was composed during the time when the events being described took place; these texts are often written by the people involved. A **secondary source** might address the same topic but provides extra commentary or analysis. These texts can be written by people not directly involved in the events. For example, a book written by a political candidate to inform people about his or her stand on an issue is a primary source; an online article written by a journalist analyzing how that position will affect the election is a secondary source.

> **Example:** "Elizabeth closed her eyes and braced herself on the armrests that divided her from her fellow passengers. Take-off was always the worst part for her. The revving of the engines, the way her stomach dropped as the plane lurched upward: it made her feel sick. Then, she had to watch the world fade away beneath her, getting smaller and smaller until it was just her and the clouds hurtling through the sky. Sometimes (but only sometimes) it just had to be endured, though. She focused on the thought of her sister's smiling face and her new baby nephew as the plane slowly pulled onto the runway."
>
> The passage above is reflective of which type of writing?
>
> a) Narrative
> b) Expository
> c) Technical
> d) Persuasive
>
> The passage is telling a story—we meet Elizabeth and learn about her fear of flying—so it's a narrative text (answer a). There is no factual information presented or explained, nor is the author trying to persuade the reader.

Facts vs. Opinions

On the PSB Reading passages you might be asked to identify a statement in a passage as either a fact or an opinion, so you'll need to know the difference between the two. A **fact** is a statement or thought that can be proven to be true. The statement *Wednesday comes after Tuesday* is a fact—you can point to a calendar to prove it. In contrast, an **opinion** is an assumption that is not based in fact and cannot be proven to be true. The assertion that *television is more entertaining than feature films* is an opinion—people will disagree on this, and there's no reference you can use to prove or disprove it.

Example:
"Exercise is critical for healthy development in children. Today, there is an epidemic of unhealthy children in the United States who will face health problems in adulthood due to poor diet and lack of exercise as children. This is a problem for all Americans, especially with the rising cost of healthcare.
"It is vital that school systems and parents encourage their children to engage in a minimum of thirty minutes of cardiovascular exercise each day, mildly increasing their heart rate for a sustained period. This is proven to decrease the likelihood of developmental diabetes, obesity, and a multitude of other health problems. Also, children need a proper diet rich in fruits and vegetables so that they can grow and develop physically, as well as learn healthy eating habits early on."

Which of the following is a fact in the passage, not an opinion?

a) Fruits and vegetables are the best way to help children be healthy.
b) Children today are lazier than they were in previous generations.
c) The risk of diabetes in children is reduced by physical activity.
d) Children should engage in thirty minutes of exercise a day.

Choice b) can be discarded immediately because it is negative and is not discussed anywhere in the passage. Answers a) and d) are both opinions—the author is promoting exercise, fruits, and vegetables as a way to make children healthy. (Notice that these incorrect answers contain words that hint at being an opinion such as *best*, *should*, or other comparisons.) Answer b), on the other hand, is a simple fact stated by the author; it's introduced by the word *proven* to indicate that you don't need to just take the author's word for it.

Drawing Conclusions

In addition to understanding the main idea and factual content of a passage, you'll also be asked to take your analysis one step further and anticipate what other information could logically be added to the passage. In a non-fiction passage, for example, you might be asked which statement the author of the passage would agree with. In an excerpt from a fictional work, you might be asked to anticipate what the character would do next.

To answer these questions, you need to have a solid understanding of the topic, theme, and main idea of the passage; armed with this information, you can figure out which of the answer choices best fits within those criteria (or alternatively, which ones do not). For example, if the author of the passage is advocating for safer working conditions in textile factories, any supporting details that would be added to the passage should support that idea. You might add sentences that contain information about the number of accidents that occur in textile factories or that outline a new plan for fire safety.

Example: "Today, there is an epidemic of unhealthy children in the United States who will face health problems in adulthood due to poor diet and lack of exercise during their childhood. This is a problem for all Americans, as adults with chronic health issues are adding to the rising cost of healthcare. A child who grows up living an unhealthy lifestyle is likely to become an adult who does the same.

"Because exercise is critical for healthy development in children, it is vital that school systems and parents encourage their children to engage in a minimum of thirty minutes of cardiovascular exercise each day. Even this small amount of exercise has been proven to decrease the likelihood that young people will develop diabetes, obesity, and other health issues as adults. In addition to exercise, children need a proper diet rich in fruits and vegetables so that they can grow and develop physically. Starting a good diet early also teaches children healthy eating habits they will carry into adulthood."

The author of this passage would most likely agree with which statement?

a) Parents are solely responsible for the health of their children.
b) Children who do not want to exercise should not be made to.
c) Improved childhood nutrition will help lower the amount Americans spend on healthcare.
d) It's not important to teach children healthy eating habits because they will learn them as adults.

The author would most likely support answer c): he mentions in the first paragraph that unhealthy habits are adding to the rising cost of healthcare. The main idea of the passage is that nutrition and exercise are important for children, so answer b) doesn't make sense—the author would likely support measures to encourage children to exercise. Answers a) and d) can also be eliminated because they are directly contradicted in the text. The author specifically mentions the role of schools systems, so he doesn't believe parents are solely responsible for their children's health. He also specifically states that children who grow up with unhealthy habit will become adults with unhealthy habits, which contradicts d).

Example: "Elizabeth closed her eyes and braced herself on the armrests that divided her from her fellow passengers. Take-off was always the worst part for her. The revving of the engines, the way her stomach dropped as the plane lurched upward: it made her feel sick. Then, she had to watch the world fade away beneath her, getting smaller and smaller until it was just her and the clouds hurtling through the sky. Sometimes (but only sometimes) it just had to be endured, though. She focused on the thought of her sister's smiling face and her new baby nephew as the plane slowly pulled onto the runway."

Which of the following is Elizabeth least likely to do in the future?

a) Take a flight to her brother's wedding.
b) Apply for a job as a flight attendant.
c) Never board an airplane again.
d) Get sick on an airplane.

It's clear from the passage that Elizabeth hates flying, but it willing to endure it for the sake of visiting her family. Thus, it seems likely that she would be willing to get on a plane for her brother's wedding, making a) and c) incorrect answers. The passage also explicitly tells us that she feels sick on planes, so d) is likely to happen. We can infer, though, that she would not enjoy being on an airplane for work, so she's very unlikely to apply for a job as a flight attendant, which is choice b).

Test Your Knowledge: Reading

Read each of the following paragraphs carefully and answer the questions that follow.

1. The Flu

Influenza, or the flu, has historically been one of the most common and deadliest human sicknesses. While many people who contract this virus will recover, others will not. Over the past 150 years, tens of millions of people have died from the flu, and millions more have been left with lingering complications including secondary infections.

Although it's a common disease, the flu is actually not highly infectious; that is, it is relatively difficult to contract. The virus can only be transmitted when individuals come into direct contact with the bodily fluids of people infected with it, often when they are exposed to expelled aerosol particles resulting from coughing and sneezing. Since these particles only travel short distances and the virus will die within a few hours on hard surfaces, it can be contained with simple health measures like hand washing and face masks.

However, the spread of this disease can only be contained when people are aware that such measures must be taken. One of the reasons the flu has historically been so deadly is the window of time between a person's infection and the development of symptoms. Viral shedding—when the body releases a virus that has been successfully reproducing in it—takes place two days after infection, while symptoms do not usually develop until the third day. Thus, infected individuals may unknowingly infect others for least twenty-four hours before developing symptoms themselves.

The Flu: Questions

1. What is the main idea of the passage?
   a) The flu is a deadly disease that's difficult to control because people become infectious before they show symptoms.
   b) In order for the flu to be transmitted, individuals must come in contact with bodily fluids from infected individuals.
   c) The spread of flu is easy to contain because the virus does not live long either as aerosol particles or on hard surfaces.
   d) The flu has killed tens of millions of people and can often cause deadly secondary infections.

2. Why isn't the flu considered to be highly infectious?
   a) Many people who get the flu will recover and have no lasting complications, so only a small number of people who become infected will die.
   b) The process of viral shedding takes two days, so infected individuals have enough time to implement simple health measures that stop the spread of the disease.
   c) The flu virus cannot travel far or live for long periods of time outside the human body, so its spread can easily be contained if measures are taken.
   d) Twenty-four hours is a relatively short period of time for the virus to spread among a population.

3. Which of the following correctly describes the flu?
    a) The flu is easy to contract and always fatal.
    b) The flu is difficult to contract and always fatal.
    c) The flu is easy to contract and sometimes fatal.
    d) The flu is difficult to contract and sometimes fatal.

4. Which statement is not a detail from the passage?
    a) Tens of millions of people have been killed by the flu virus.
    b) There is typically a twenty-four hour window during which individuals are infectious but not showing flu symptoms.
    c) Viral shedding is the process by which people recover from the flu.
    d) The flu can be transmitted by direct contact with bodily fluids from infected individuals or by exposure to aerosol particles.

5. What is the meaning of the word measures in the last paragraph?
    a) a plan of action
    b) a standard unit
    c) an adequate amount
    d) a rhythmic movement

6. What can the reader conclude from the passage above?
    a) Preemptively implementing health measures like hand washing and face masks could help stop the spread of the flu virus.
    b) Doctors are not sure how the flu virus is transmitted, so they are unsure how to stop it from spreading.
    c) The flu is dangerous because it is both deadly and highly infectious.
    d) Individuals stop being infectious three days after they are infected.

2. Snakes

Skin coloration and markings play an important role in the world of snakes. Those intricate diamonds, stripes, and swirls help these animals hide from predators and attract mates. Perhaps most importantly (for us humans, anyway), the markings can also indicate whether a snake is venomous. While it might seem counterintuitive for a poisonous snake to stand out in bright red or blue, that fancy costume tells any approaching predator that eating it would be a bad idea.

If you see a flashy-looking snake out the woods, though, those markings don't necessarily mean it's poisonous: some snakes have a found a way to ward off predators without the actual venom. The California king snake, for example, has very similar markings to the venomous coral snake with whom it frequently shares a habitat. However, the king snake is actually nonvenomous; it's merely pretending to be dangerous to eat. A predatory hawk or eagle, usually hunting from high in the sky, can't tell the difference between the two species, so the king snake gets passed over and lives another day.

Snakes: Questions

7. What is the author's primary purpose in writing this essay?
    a) to explain how the markings on a snake are related to whether it is venomous
    b) to teach readers the difference between coral snakes and king snakes
    c) to illustrate why snakes are dangerous
    d) to demonstrate how animals survive in difficult environments

8. What can the reader conclude from the passage above?
    a) The king snake is dangerous to humans.
    b) The coral snake and the king snake are both hunted by the same predators.
    c) It's safe to handle snakes in the woods because you can easily tell whether they're poisonous.
    d) The king snake changes its markings when hawks or eagles are close by.

9. What is the best summary of this passage?
    a) Humans can use coloration and markings to determine whether snakes are poisonous.
    b) Animals often use coloration and markings to attract mates and warn predators that they're poisonous.
    c) The California king snake and coral snake have nearly identical markings.
    d) Venomous snakes often have bright markings, although nonvenomous snakes can also mimic those colors.

10. Which statement is not a detail from the passage?
    a) Predators will avoid eating king snakes because their markings are similar to those on coral snakes.
    b) King snakes and coral snakes live in the same habitats.
    c) The coral snake uses its coloration to hide from predators.
    d) The king snake is not venomous.

11. What is the meaning of the word intricate in the first paragraph?
    a) complicated
    b) colorful
    c) purposeful
    d) changeable

12. What is the difference between king snakes and coral snakes according to the passage?
    a) Both king snakes and coral snakes are nonvenomous, but coral snakes have colorful markings.
    b) Both king snakes and coral snakes are venomous, but king snakes have colorful markings.
    c) King snakes are nonvenomous, while coral snakes are venomous.
    d) Coral snakes are nonvenomous, while king snakes are venomous.

3. Taking Temperatures

Taking a person's temperature is one of the most basic and common health care tasks. Everyone from nurses to emergency medical technicians to concerned parents has needed to grab a thermometer and take somebody's temperature. But what is the best way to get an accurate reading? The answer depends on the situation.

The most common way people measure body temperature is orally. A simple digital or disposable thermometer is placed under the tongue for a few minutes, and the task is complete. There are many situations, however, when measuring temperature orally isn't an option. For example, when a person can't breathe through his nose, he won't be able to keep his mouth closed long enough to get an accurate reading. In these situations, it's often preferable to place the thermometer in the rectum or armpit. In addition, using the rectum provides a much more accurate reading than any other location does.

It's also often the case that certain people, like agitated patients or fussy babies, won't be able to sit still long enough for an accurate reading. In these situations, it's best to use a thermometer that works much more quickly, such as one that measures temperature in the ear or at the temporal artery. No matter which method is chosen, however, it's important to check the average temperature for each region, as it can vary by several degrees.

Taking Temperatures: Questions

13. Which statement is not a detail from the passage?
    a) Taking someone's temperature in her ear or at her temporal artery is more accurate than taking it orally.
    b) If an individual cannot breathe through his nose, taking his temperature orally will likely result in an inaccurate reading.
    c) The standard human body temperature varies depending on whether it's measured in the mouth, rectum, armpit, ear, or temporal artery.
    d) The most common way to measure temperature is by placing a thermometer in the mouth.

14. What is the author's primary purpose in writing this essay?
    a) to advocate for the use of thermometers that measure temperature in the ear or at the temporal artery
    b) to explain the methods available to measure a person's temperature and the situations in which each method is appropriate
    c) to warn readers that the average temperature of the human body varies by region
    d) to discuss how nurses use different types of thermometers depending on the patient they are examining

15. What is the best summary of this passage?
    a) It's important that everyone knows the best way to take a person's temperature in any given situation.
    b) The most common method of taking a person's temperature—orally—isn't appropriate in some situations.
    c) The most accurate way to take a temperature is by placing a digital thermometer in the rectum.
    d) It's important to check a person's temperature in more than one region of the body.

16. What is the meaning of the word agitated in the last paragraph?

a) obviously upset
b) quickly moving
c) violently ill
d) slightly dirty

17. According to the passage, why is it sometimes preferable to take a person's temperature rectally?

a) Rectal readings are more accurate than oral readings.
b) Many people cannot sit still long enough to have their temperatures taken orally.
c) Temperature readings can vary widely between regions of the body.
d) Many people do not have access to fast-acting thermometers.

Test Your Knowledge: Reading – Answers

1. a)
2. c)
3. d)
4. c)
5. a)
6. a)
7. a)
8. b)
9. d)
10. c)
11. a)
12. c)
13. a)
14. b)
15. b)
16. a)
17. a)

Chapter 5: Natural Sciences

The PSB-HOAE Science test measures your knowledge of the life sciences and physical sciences: Chemistry, Biology, and Physics. Although we can't cover 12 years of schooling – not without a much larger book, anyway! – this section will refresh your memory on the necessary fundamental science principles. Take particular note to the bold faced words. These are the terms most commonly seen on the test. Here's a breakdown of areas covered:

1. **Biology**
    - Basics of Life
    - Cellular Respiration
    - Classification of Organisms
    - Microorganisms
    - Animals
    - Plants
    - Ecology
    - Cells, Tissues, and Organs
    - Reproduction
    - Heredity
    - The Systems of the Body: Circulatory; Respiratory; Skeletal; Nervous; Muscular; Digestive; Renal

2. **Chemistry**
    - Elements, Compounds, and Mixtures
    - States of Matter
    - The Periodic Table and Chemical Bonds
    - Acids and Bases

3. **Physics**
    - Motion
    - Thermal Physics
    - Heat Transfer
    - Wave Motion (Sound) and Magnetism

Biology

This section covers the basics of biology, from the building blocks of life, to the fundamentals of biological chemistry and the classification of organisms.

BASICS OF LIFE

We began learning the difference between living (**animate**) beings and nonliving (**inanimate**) objects from an early age. Living organisms and inanimate objects are all composed of **atoms** from elements. Those atoms are arranged into groups called **molecules**, which serve as the building blocks of everything in existence (as we know it). Molecular interactions are what determine whether something is classified as animate or inanimate. The following is a list of the most commonly-found elements found in the molecules of animate beings:

- Oxygen
- Carbon
- Sodium
- Magnesium
- Iodine
- Sulfur
- Potassium
- Chlorine
- Nitrogen
- Calcium
- Phosphorous
- Iron
- Hydrogen

Another way to describe living and nonliving things is through the terms **organic** and **inorganic.**

- **Organic molecules** are from living organisms. Organic molecules contain **carbon-hydrogen bonds**.

- **Inorganic molecules** come from non-living resources. They do not contain carbon-hydrogen bonds.

There are four major classes of organic molecules:

1. **Carbohydrates**

2. **Lipids**

3. **Proteins**

4. **Nucleic acids**.

Carbohydrates

Carbohydrates consist of only hydrogen, oxygen, and carbon atoms. They are the most abundant single class of organic substances found in nature. Carbohydrate molecules provide many basic necessities such as: fiber, vitamins, and minerals; structural components for organisms, especially plants; and, perhaps most importantly, energy. Our bodies break down carbohydrates to make **glucose**: a sugar used to produce that energy which our bodies need in order to operate. Brain cells are exclusively dependent upon a constant source of glucose molecules.

There are two kinds of carbohydrates: simple and complex.

Simple carbohydrates can be absorbed directly through the cell, and therefore enter the blood stream very quickly. We consume simple carbohydrates in dairy products, fruits, and other sugary foods.

Complex carbohydrates consist of a chain of simple sugars which, over time, our bodies break down into simple sugars (which are also referred to as stored energy.) **Glycogen** is the storage form of glucose in human and animal cells. Complex carbohydrates come from starches like cereal, bread, beans, potatoes, and starchy vegetables.

Lipids

Lipids, commonly known as fats, are molecules with two functions:

1. They are stored as an energy reserve.

2. They provide a protective cushion for vital organs.

In addition to those two functions, lipids also combine with other molecules to form essential compounds, such as **phospholipids,** which form the membranes around cells. Lipids also combine with other molecules to create naturally-occurring **steroid** hormones, like the hormones estrogen and testosterone.

Proteins

Proteins are large molecules which our bodies' cells need in order to function properly. Consisting of **amino acids,** proteins aid in maintaining and creating many aspects of our cells: cellular structure, function, and regulation, to name a few. Proteins also work as neurotransmitters and carriers of oxygen in the blood (hemoglobin).

Without protein, our tissues and organs could not exist. Our muscles bones, skin, and many other parts of the body contain significant amounts of protein. **Enzymes**, hormones, and antibodies are proteins.

Enzymes
When heat is applied, chemical reactions are typically sped up. However, the amount of heat required to speed up reactions could be potentially harmful (even fatal) to living organisms. Instead, our bodies use molecules called enzymes to bring reactants closer together, causing them to form a new compound. Thus, the whole reaction rate is increased without heat. Even better – the enzymes are not consumed during the reaction process, and can therefore be used reused. This makes them an important biochemical part of both photosynthesis and respiration.

Nucleic Acid

Nucleic acids are large molecules made up of smaller molecules called **nucleotides. DNA** (deoxyribonucleic acid) transports and transmits genetic information. As you can tell from the name, DNA is a nucleic acid. Since nucleotides make up nucleic acids, they are considered the basis of reproduction and progression.

Test Your Knowledge: Basics of Life

1. Life depends upon:
   a) The bond energy in molecules.
   b) The energy of protons.
   c) The energy of electrons.
   d) The energy of neutrons.

2. Which of the following elements is **NOT** found in carbohydrates?
   a) Carbon.
   b) Hydrogen.
   c) Oxygen.
   d) Sulfur.

3. Which of the following is a carbohydrate molecule?
   a) Amino acid.
   b) Glycogen.
   c) Sugar.
   d) Lipid.

4. Lipids are commonly known as:
   a) Fat.
   b) Sugar.
   c) Enzymes.
   d) Protein.

5. Proteins are composed of:
   a) Nucleic acids.
   b) Amino acids.
   c) Hormones.
   d) Lipids.

Test Your Knowledge: Basics of Life – Answers

1. a)

2. d)

3. c)

4. a)

5. b)

CELLULAR RESPIRATION

As you can imagine, there are a great deal of processes which require energy: breathing, blood circulation, body temperature control, muscle usage, digestion, brain and nerve functioning are all only a few examples. You can refer to all of the body's physical and chemical processes which convert or use energy as **metabolism**.

All living things in the world, including plants, require energy in order to maintain their metabolisms. Initially, that energy is consumed through food. That energy is processed in plants and animals through **photosynthesis** (for plants) and **respiration** (for animals). **Cellular respiration** produces the actual energy molecules known as **ATP** (Adenosine Tri-Phosphate) molecules.

Plants use ATP during **photosynthesis** for producing glucose, which is then broken down during cellular respiration. This cycle continuously repeats itself throughout the life of the plant.

Photosynthesis: Plants, as well as some Protists and Monerans, can use light energy to bind together small molecules from the environment. These newly-bound molecules are then used as fuel to make more energy. This process is called photosynthesis, and one of its byproducts is none other than oxygen. Most organisms, including plants, require oxygen to fuel the biochemical reactions of metabolism.

You can see in the following equation that plants use the energy taken from light to turn carbon dioxide and water – the small molecules from their environment – into glucose and oxygen.

The photosynthesis equation:

$$\mathbf{CO2 \;+\; H2O \xrightarrow{\text{Light}} C6H12O6 \;+\; O2}$$

CO2	+	H2O	Light ⟶	C6H12O6	+	O2
Carbon Dioxide		Water		Glucose (sugar)		Oxygen

Chlorophyll

In order for photosynthesis to occur, however, plants require a specific molecule to capture sunlight. This molecule is called **chlorophyll**. When chlorophyll absorbs sunlight, one of its electrons is stimulated into a higher energy state. This higher-energy electron then passes that energy onto other electrons in other molecules, creating a chain that eventually results in glucose. Chlorophyll absorbs red and blue light, but not green; green light is reflected off of plants, which is why plants appear green to us. It's important to note that chlorophyll is absolutely necessary to the photosynthesis process in plants –if it photosynthesizes, it will have chlorophyll.

The really fascinating aspect of photosynthesis is that raw sunlight energy is a very nonliving thing; however, it is still absorbed by plants to form the chemical bonds between simple inanimate compounds. This produces organic sugar, which is the chemical basis for the formation of all living compounds. Isn't it amazing? Something nonliving is essential to the creation of all living things!

Respiration

Respiration is the metabolic opposite of photosynthesis. There are two types of respiration: **aerobic** (which uses oxygen) and **anaerobic** (which occurs without the use of oxygen).

You may be confused at thinking of the word "respiration" in this way, since many people use respiration to refer to the process of breathing. However, in biology, breathing is thought of as **inspiration** (inhaling) and **expiration** (exhalation); whereas **respiration** is the metabolic, chemical reaction supporting these processes. Both plants and animals produce carbon dioxide through respiration.

Aerobic respiration is the reaction which uses enzymes to combine oxygen with organic matter (food). This yields carbon dioxide, water, and energy.

The respiration equation looks like this:

$$C6H12O6 + 6O2 \xrightarrow{\textbf{Enzymes}} 7\ 6CO2 + 6H2O + \text{energy}$$

If you look back the equation for photosynthesis, you will see that respiration is almost the same equation, only it goes in the opposite direction. (Photosynthesis uses carbon dioxide and water, with the help of energy, to create oxygen and glucose. Respiration uses oxygen and glucose, with the help of enzymes, to create carbon dioxide, water, and energy.)

Anaerobic respiration is respiration that occurs WITHOUT the use of oxygen. It produces less energy than aerobic respiration produces, yielding only two molecules of ATP per glucose molecule Aerobic respiration produces 38 ATP per glucose molecule.

So, plants convert energy into matter and release oxygen gas – animals then absorb this oxygen gas in order to run their own metabolic reaction and, in the process, release carbon dioxide. That carbon dioxide is then absorbed by plants in the photosynthetic conversion of energy into matter. Everything comes full circle! This is called a **metabolic cycle.**

Test Your Knowledge: Cellular Respiration

1. Which of the following is **NOT** true of enzymes?
   a) Enzymes are lipid molecules.
   b) Enzymes are not consumed in a biochemical reaction.
   c) Enzymes are important in photosynthesis and respiration.
   d) Enzymes speed up reactions and make them more efficient.

2. Plants appear green because chlorophyll:
   a) Absorbs green light.
   b) Reflects red light.
   c) Absorbs blue light.
   d) Reflects green light.

3. Photosynthesis is the opposite of:
   a) Enzymatic hydrolysis.
   b) Protein synthesis.
   c) Respiration.
   d) Reproduction.

4. The compound that absorbs light energy during photosynthesis is:
   a) Chloroform.
   b) Chlorofluorocarbon.
   c) Chlorinated biphenyls.
   d) Chlorophyll.

5. What is the name of the sugar molecule produced during photosynthesis?
   a) Chlorophyll
   b) Glycogen
   c) Glucose
   d) Fructose

Test Your Knowledge: Cellular Respiration – Answers

1. a)

2. d)

3. c)

4. d)

5. c)

CLASSIFICATION OF ORGANISMS

All of Earth's organisms have characteristics which distinguish them from one another. Scientists have developed systems to organize and classify all of Earth's organisms based on those characteristics.

Kingdoms

Through the process of evolution, organisms on Earth have developed into many diverse forms, which have complex relationships. Scientists have organized life into five large groups called **kingdoms**. Each kingdom contains those organisms that share significant characteristics distinguishing them from organisms in other kingdoms. These five kingdoms are named as follows:

1. **Animalia**
2. **Plantae**
3. **Fungi**
4. **Protista**
5. **Monera**

Kingdom Animalia

This kingdom contains multicellular organisms multicellular, or those known as complex organisms. These organisms are generically called **heterotrophs**, which means that they must eat preexisting organic matter (either plants or other animals) in order to sustain themselves.

Those heterotrophs which eat only plants are called **herbivores** (from "herbo," meaning "herb" or "plant"); those that kill and eat other animals for food are called **carnivores** (from "carno," meaning "flesh" or "meat"); and still other animals eat both plants *and* other animals – they are called **omnivores** (from "omnis," which means "all").

Those organisms in the Animal Kingdom have nervous tissue which has developed into nervous systems and brains; they are also able to move from place to place using muscular systems. The Animal Kingdom is divided into two groups: **vertebrates** (with backbones) and **invertebrates** (without backbones).

Kingdom Plantae

As you can guess from its name, the Plant Kingdom contains all plant-based life. Plants are multicellular organisms that use chlorophyll, which is held in specialized cellular structures called **chloroplasts,** to capture sunlight energy. Remember: photosynthesis! They then convert that sunlight energy into organic matter: their food. Because of this, most plants are referred to as **autotrophs** (self-feeders). There are a few organisms included in the Plant Kingdom which are not multicellular – certain types of algae which, while not multicellular, have cells with a nucleus. These algae also contain chlorophyll.

Except for algae, most plants are divided into one of two groups: **vascular plants** (most crops, trees, and flowering plants) and **nonvascular plants** (mosses). Vascular plants have specialized tissue that allows them to transport water and nutrients from their roots, to their leaves, and back again – even when the plant is several hundred feet tall. Nonvascular plants cannot do this, and therefore remain very small in size. Vascular plants are able to grow in both wet and dry environments; whereas nonvascular plants, since they are unable to transport water, are usually found only in wet, marshy areas.

Kingdom Fungi

The Fungi Kingdom contains organisms that share some similarities with plants, but also have other characteristics that make them more animal-like. For example, they resemble animals in that they lack chlorophyll – so they can't perform photosynthesis. This means that they don't produce their own food and are therefore heterotrophs.

However, they resemble plants in that they reproduce by spores; they also resemble plants in appearance. The bodies of fungi are made of filaments called **hyphae**, which in turn create the tissue **mycelium.** The most well-known examples of organisms in this Kingdom are mushrooms, yeasts, and molds. Fungi are very common and benefit other organisms, including humans.

Kingdom Protista

This kingdom includes single-celled organisms that contain a nucleus as part of their structure. They are considered a simple cell, but still contain multiple structures and accomplish many functions. This Kingdom includes organisms such as paramecium, amoeba, and slime molds. They often move around using hair-like structures called *cilia* or *flagellums.*

Kingdom Monera

This kingdom contains only bacteria. All of these organisms are single-celled and do not have a nucleus. They have only one chromosome, which is used to transfer genetic information. Sometimes they can also transmit genetic information using small structures called **plasmids.** Like organisms in the Protista Kingdom, they use flagella to move. Bacteria usually reproduce asexually.

There are more forms of bacteria than any other organism on Earth. Some bacteria are beneficial to us, like the ones found in yogurt; others can cause us to get sick such as the bacteria *E. coli.*

Kingdom	Description	Examples
Animalia	Multi-celled; parasites; prey; consumers; can be herbivorous, carnivorous, or omnivorous	Sponges, worms, insects, fish, mammals, reptiles, birds, humans
Plantae	Multi-celled; autotrophs; mostly producers	Ferns, angiosperms, gymnosperms, mosses
Fungi	Can be single or multi-celled; decomposers; parasites; absorb food; asexual; consumers	Mushrooms, mildew, molds, yeast
Protista	Single or multi-celled; absorb food; both producers and consumers	Plankton, algae, amoeba, protozoans
Monera	Single-celled or a colony of single-cells; decomposers and parasites; move in water; are both producers and consumers	Bacteria, blue-green algae

Levels of Classification

Kingdom groupings are not very specific. They contain organisms defined by broad characteristics, and which may not seem similar at all. For example, worms belong in Kingdom Animalia – but then, so do birds. These two organisms are very different, despite sharing the necessary traits to make it into the animal kingdom. Therefore, to further distinguish different organisms, we have multiple levels of classification, which gradually become more specific until we finally reach the actual organism.

We generally start out by grouping organisms into the appropriate kingdom. Within each kingdom, we have other subdivisions: **Phylum, Class, Order, Family, Genus, and Species.** (In some cases, "Species" can be further narrowed down into "Sub-Species.")

As we move down the chain, characteristics become more specific, and the number of organisms in each group decreases. For an example, let's try to classify a grizzly bear. The chart would go as follows:

Kingdom - insect, fish, bird, pig, dog, bear

Phylum - fish, bird, pig, dog, bear

Class - pig, dog, bear

Order - dog, bear

Family -panda,brown,grizzly

Genus - brown, grizzly

Species - grizzly

Here is an easy way to remember the order of terms used in this classification scheme:

Kings **P**lay **C**ards **O**n **F**riday, **G**enerally **S**peaking.
Kingdom, **P**hylum, **C**lass, **O**rder, **F**amily, **G**enus, **S**pecies

Binomial Nomenclature

Organisms can be positively identified by two Latin words. Therefore, the organism naming system is referred to as a binomial nomenclature ("binomial" referring to the number two, and "nomenclature" referring to a title or name). Previously-used words help illustrate where the organism fits into the whole scheme, but it is only the last two, the genus and species, that specifically name an organism. Both are written in italics. The genus is always capitalized, but the species name is written lowercase.

Grizzly bears fall underneath the genus *Ursus*, species *arctos*, and sub-species *horribilis*. Therefore, the scientific name of the grizzly bear would be *Ursus arctos horribilis. Canis familiaris* is the scientific name for a common dog, *Felis domesticus* is a common cat, and humans are *Homo sapiens*.

Test Your Knowledge: Classification of Organisms

1. Which feature distinguishes those organisms in Kingdom Monera from those in other kingdoms? Organisms in Kingdom Monera:
   a) Contain specialized organelles.
   b) Contain a nucleus.
   c) Contain chloroplasts.
   d) Lack a nucleus.

2. Which of the following has the classification levels in the correct order, from most general to most specific?
   a) Kingdom, Phylum, Class, Order, Family, Genus, Species.
   b) Order, Family, Genus, Species, Class, Phylum, Kingdom.
   c) Species, Genus, Family, Order, Class, Phylum, Kingdom.
   d) Kingdom, Phylum, Class, Species, Genus, Family, Order.

3. The ___________contains organisms with both plant-and-animal-like characteristics?
   a) Animal Kingdom.
   b) Plant Kingdom.
   c) Fungi Kingdom.
   d) Monera Kingdom.

4. Which of the following kingdom's members are multicellular AND autotrophic?
   a) Fungi.
   b) Animalia.
   c) Protista.
   d) Plantae.

5. Which of the following kingdom's members have tissue called hyphae?
   a) Fungi.
   b) Animalia.
   c) Protista.
   d) Plantae.

Test Your Knowledge: Classification of Organisms – Answers

1. **d)**
2. **a)**
3. **c)**
4. **d)**
5. **a)**

MICROORGANISMS

Microorganisms (microbes) are extremely small and cannot be seen with the naked eye. They can be detected using either a microscope or through various chemical tests. These organisms are everywhere, even in such extreme environments as very hot areas, very cold areas, dry areas, and deep in the ocean under tremendous pressure. Some of these organisms cause diseases in animals, plants, and humans. However, most are helpful to us and the Earth's ecosystems. In fact, we are totally dependent upon microbes for our quality of life. There are three types of microorganisms: **bacteria, protists, and fungi.**

Bacteria

Bacteria are microorganisms that do not have a true nucleus; their genetic material simply floats around in the cell. They are very small, simple, one-celled organisms. Bacteria are normally found in three variations: **bacilli** (rod-shaped), **cocci** (sphere-shaped), and **spirilla** (spiral-shaped). Bacteria are widespread in all environments and are important participants within all ecosystems. They are **decomposers**, because they break down dead organic matter into basic molecules.

Bacteria are also an important part of the food-chain, because they are eaten by other organisms. Still, bacteria remain the most numerous organisms on Earth. This is due to the fact that they are small, can live practically anywhere, and have great metabolic flexibility. But most importantly, bacteria have the ability to rapidly reproduce. In thc right environment, any bacteria can reproduce every 20 or 30 minutes, each one doubling after each reproduction.

Benefits of Bacteria – Some bacteria are found in our intestinal tracts, where they help to digest our food and make vitamins.

To demonstrate the significance of bacteria, let's look at the cycle of nitrogen, which is used by organisms to make proteins. The cycle starts with dead plants being decomposed by bacteria. The nitrogen from the plant tissue is released into the atmosphere, where nitrifying bacteria convert that nitrogen into ammonia-type compounds. Other bacteria act upon these compounds to form nitrates for plants to absorb. When these new plants die, we are brought back again to the decomposing bacteria releasing the plant's nitrogen into the atmosphere.

Bacterial Diseases - Microorganisms, including bacteria, enter our bodies in a variety of ways: through the air we breathe, ingestion by mouth, or through the skin via a cut or injury. We can eliminate much of this threat by disinfecting utensils and thoroughly washing our hands. This destroys bacteria and other microorganisms which may cause disease.

Protists

Protists are very diversified and include organisms that range greatly in size – from single cells to considerably complex structures, some longer than 100 meters. Protists have a wide variety of reproductive and nutritional strategies, and their genetic material is enclosed within a nucleus. Even though protists are more simplistic than other organisms with cellular nuclei, they are not as primitive as bacteria.

Some are autotrophic and contain chlorophyll; others are heterotrophic and consume other organisms to survive. Because protists obtain food in both of these ways, it is generally believed that early protists were both animal- and plant-like. Protists are important to food chains and ecosystems, although some protists do cause disease.

Fungi

Fungi are heterotrophic and can be either single-celled or multi-celled. They play an important decomposition role in an ecosystem, because they consume dead organic matter. This returns nutrients to the soil for eventual uptake by plants.

There are three types of fungi which obtain food: saprophytic, parasitic, and mycorrhizal-associated.

Saprophytic fungi consume dead organic matter; **parasitic** fungi attack living plants and animals; and **mycorrhizal-associated** fungi form close relationships (**symbiosis**) with trees, shrubs, and other plants, where each partner in the relationship mutually benefits. An organism called **lichen** is an example of a symbiotic union between a fungus and algae.

Fungi produce **spores** (reproductive structures) that are highly resistant to extreme temperatures and moisture levels. This gives them the ability to survive for a long time, even in aggressive environments. When their environments become more favorable, the spores **germinate** (sprout) and grow. Spores are able to travel to new areas, which spreads the organism. Fungi absorb food through **hyphae**. A large mass of joined, branched hyphae is called the **mycelium**, which constitutes the main body of the multicellular fungi. However, the mycelium is not usually seen, because it is hidden throughout the food source which is being consumed. The largest organism in the world is believed to be a soil fungus whose mycelium tissue extends for many acres!

What we do usually see of a fungus is the fungal fruiting body. A mushroom is a fruiting body filled with spores. The main body of the mushroom (the **mycelium**) is under the soil surface.

Test Your Knowledge: Microorganisms

1. Fungi are decomposers, which is important for______________.

a) Making nutrients available for recycling back into the soil.
b) Producing oxygen by photosynthesizing.
c) Producing oxygen by respiration.
d) Living in mostly aquatic environments.

2. Which is the most numerous organism on Earth?

a) Paramecium from the Protist Kingdom.
b) Yeast from the Fungi Kingdom.
c) Euglena from the Protist Kingdom.
d) Bacteria from the Moneran Kingdom.

3. Which kingdom contains organisms that are able to convert atmospheric nitrogen to nitrate?

a) Animalia.
b) Plantae.
c) Monera.
d) Protista.

4. Why are spores produced?

a) They are part of resistance.
b) To reproduce.
c) To photosynthesize.
d) They are part of the support system.

5. Members of the Kingdom Monera are found in our digestive tracts and perform which of the following functions?

a) Produce carbohydrates.
b) Produce vitamins.
c) Produce lipids.
d) Produce proteins.

Test Your Knowledge: Microorganisms – Answers

1. **a)**
2. **d)**
3. **c)**
4. **b)**
5. **b)**

ANIMALS

Animals are multi-celled and unable to produce their own food internally, just like plants. As mentioned previously, the Animal Kingdom is divided into two large groupings: the **invertebrates** and **vertebrates.**

Invertebrates are multicellular, have no back bone or cell walls, reproduce sexually, and are heterotrophic. They make up approximately 97% of the animal population.

Vertebrates, on the other hand, have well-developed internal skeletons, highly developed brains, an advanced nervous system, and an outer covering of protective cellular skin. They make up the remaining 3% of the animals.

What Is an Animal?

All animals, from sponges to human beings, share some fundamental characteristics. One such characteristic is cellular division. At the beginning of reproduction, an egg is fertilized and then undergoes several cell divisions (cleavages); this process quickly produces a cluster of cells. Cell division continues through many distinct stages before finally resulting in an embryo. The full, multi-celled organism then develops tissues and organ systems, eventually developing into its adult form.

All multicellular animals must come up with solutions to several basic problems:

- **Surface-area-to-volume issues:** Nutrients, air, and water must be able to enter an animal's body in order to sustain life; therefore, the surface area of an animal's body must be large enough to allow a sufficient amount of these elements to be consumed by the organism. In single-celled organisms, the cell size is limited to the amount of nutrients able to pass through the cell membrane to support the cell. In multi-celled organisms, specialized tissues and organ systems with very large surface areas bring in the necessary elements and then carry them to the cells. Those specialized tissues are found in the respiratory system, urinary system, excretory system, and the digestive system. These tissues and organs, along with the circulatory system, are able to support a large-sized body.

- **Body support and protection:** All animals have some form of support and protection in the form of their internal or external skeletal systems. These skeletal systems provide support for the animal's body and protect the internal organs from damage.

- **Mobility:** Animals are heterotrophs and must acquire food; this need, along with the need to mate and reproduce, requires the animal to move. Although plants move, they are considered stationary because they are rooted. Animals, on the other hand, move from place to place; this is called **locomotion.** Locomotion requires a muscular system. Muscles are found only in animals; they are not present in plants, fungi, or single-celled microorganisms.

- **Sensory integration**: Animals have many specialized sensory organs: eyes, ears, noses, etc. These organs make animals aware of the environment and give them the ability to respond to environmental stimuli. The integration and coordination of sense organs with other bodily functions requires an organized collection of specialized nervous tissue, known as a **central nervous system** (CNS).

A Few Animal Phyla

Phylum Porifera: Sponges.
Collections of individual cells with no tissues or organs, and no nervous system or skeleton.

Phylum Coelenterata: Jellyfish, sea anemones, and coral.
Bodies symmetrical in a circular fashion with rudimentary organs and systems, but no skeleton.

Phylum Echinodermata: Sea stars and sea urchins.
Bodies have circular symmetry with five body parts arranged around a central axis. They have calcium spines or plates just under the skin.

Phylum Mollusca: Snails, clams, and octopi.
These have a well-developed circulatory system, nervous system, and digestive system; octopuses have particularly well-developed brains.

Phylum Arthropoda: Crustaceans, spiders, and insects.
This phylum has more species than the other phyla. They have exoskeletons, and most undergo **metamorphosis** (a physical transformation that is a part of the growth process). They often have specialized body parts (antennae, pinchers, etc.), and they are well adapted to many environments.

Phylum Chordata: Amphibians, reptiles, fish, birds, and mammals (including humans).
All share four characteristics: a notochord that develops into the vertebral column in vertebrates, a nerve cord that runs along the spinal column, gill slits at some point in our development, and a tail or at least a vestigial tail (humans have the tailbone or coccyx).

Test Your Knowledge: Animals

1. Multicellular animals have developed respiratory and excretory systems to overcome which of the following issues?
    a) Weight versus mass.
    b) Surface-area-to-volume.
    c) Height to weight.
    d) Mass to volume.

2. The two categories of animals are:
    a) Single-celled and multi-celled.
    b) Autotrophic and heterotrophic.
    c) Those that live in water and those that live on land.
    d) Vertebrate and invertebrate.

3. Jellyfish and coral are related to:
    a) Octopi.
    b) Sea anemones.
    c) Sea urchins.
    d) Sponges.

4. The Phylum Arthropoda contains which of the following animals?
    a) Spiders.
    b) Sea stars.
    c) Sponges.
    d) Seals.

5. Humans are classified under which of the following Phyla?
    a) Echinodermata.
    b) Chordata.
    c) Mollusca.
    d) Platyhelminthes.

Test Your Knowledge: Animals – Answers

1. **b)**

2. **d)**

3. **b)**

4. **a)**

5. **b)**

Chemistry

General chemistry examines the structure of matter and the reaction between matter and energy. It is the science that deals with the properties and transformation of materials. This section will cover the fundamental terms and processes of general chemistry including states of matter, chemical bonds, the periodic table, principles and applications.

ELEMENTS, COMPOUNDS, and MIXTURES

Matter

Matter is commonly defined as anything that takes up space and has mass. **Mass** is the quantity of matter something possesses, and usually has a unit of weight associated with it.

Matter can undergo two types of change: chemical and physical.

> A **chemical change** occurs when an original substance is transformed into a new substance with different properties. An example would be the burning of wood, which produces ash and smoke.
>
> Transformations that do not produce new substances, such as stretching a rubber band or melting ice, are called **physical changes**.

The fundamental properties which we use to measure matter are mass, weight, volume, density and specific gravity.

Extrinsic properties are directly related to the amount of material being measured, such as weight and volume.

Intrinsic properties are those which are independent of the quantity of matter present, such as density and specific gravity.

Atom

An atom is the ultimate particle of matter; it is the smallest particle of an element that still is a part of that element. All atoms of the same element have the same mass. Atomic chemical changes involve the transfer of whole atoms from one substance to another; but atoms are not created or destroyed in ordinary chemical changes.

An atom is made up of several parts. The center is called the **nucleus**, and is made up of two particles: a positively-charged particle, called a **proton,** and a particle that does not have a charge, called a **neutron**. The masses of a proton and neutron are about the same.

The nucleus of the atom is surrounded by negatively-charged particles called **electrons**, which move in orbits around the nucleus. The nucleus is only a small portion of the total amount of space an atom takes up, even though most of an atom's mass is contained in the nucleus.

Molecular Weight

A **mole** is the amount of substance that contains 6.02 x 10^{23} basic particles. This is referred to as **Avogadro's number** and is based on the number of atoms in C_{12} (Carbon 12). For example, a mole of copper is the amount of copper that contains exactly 6.02 x 10^{23} atoms, and one mole of water contains 6.02 x 10^{23} H_2O molecules. The weight of one mole of an element is called its **atomic weight**. The atomic weight of an element with isotopes, which are explained further on the next page, is the average of the isotopes' individual atomic weights.

The negatively-charged electrons are very light in mass. An atom is described as neutral if it has an equal number of protons and electrons, or if the number of electrons is the same as the atomic number of the atom. You may have already assumed –correctly! – from that information that the atomic number of an atom equals the number of protons in that atom. The **atomic weight** or **mass** of the atom is the total number of protons and neutrons in the atom's nucleus.

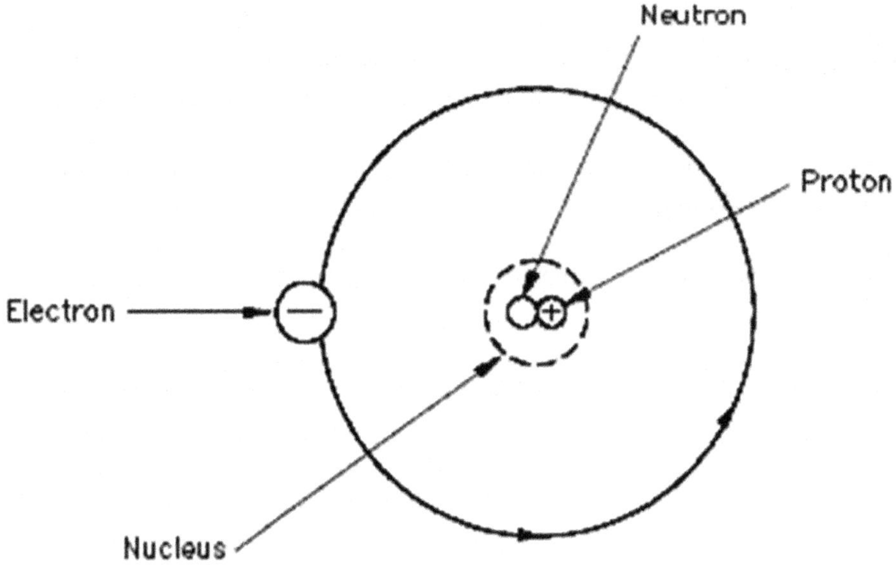

[1]

Elements

An element is a substance which cannot be broken down by chemical means; they are composed of atoms that have the same **atomic number** and are defined by the number of protons and neutrons they have. Some elements have more than one form, such as carbon; these alternate forms are called **isotopes.** There are approximately 109 known elements. Eighty-eight of these occur naturally on earth, while the others are **synthesized** (manufactured).

Hydrogen is the most abundant element in the Universe. It is found in 75% of all matter known to exist. **Helium** is the second most abundant element, found in approximately 25% of all known matter. The Earth is composed mostly of iron, oxygen, silicon, and magnesium, though these elements are not evenly

[1] Graphic from: http://www.circuitlab.org

distributed. 90% of the human body's mass consists of oxygen, carbon, hydrogen, nitrogen, calcium, and phosphorus. 75% of elements are metals, and eleven are gases in their natural state. We'll cover this more in-depth when we view the periodic table.

Molecules

A molecule is the smallest part of a substance that isn't chemically bonded to another atom. **Chemical formulas** are used to represent the atomic composition of a molecule. For example, one molecule of water contains 2 atoms of Hydrogen and 1 atom of Oxygen; its chemical formula is $\mathbf{2H + O = H_2O}$.

Compounds and Mixtures

Substances that contain more than one type of element are called **compounds.** Compounds that are made up of molecules which are all identical are called **pure substances**. A **mixture** consists of two or more substances that are not chemically bonded. Mixtures are generally placed in one of two categories:

> **Homogeneous Mixture**: Components that make up the mixture are uniformly distributed; examples are water and air.
>
> **Heterogeneous Mixture**: Components of the mixture are not uniform; they sometimes have localized regions with different properties. For example: the different components of soup makc it a heterogeneous mixture. Rocks, as well, are not uniform and have localized regions with different properties.

A uniform, or homogenous, mixture of different molecules is called a **solution**. If the solution is a liquid, the material being dissolved is the **solute** and the liquid it is being dissolved in is called the **solvent.** Both solids and gases can dissolve in liquids. A **saturated** has reached a point of maximum concentration; in it, no more solute will dissolve.

Test Your Knowledge: Elements, Compounds, and Mixtures

1. Which statement describe the nucleus of an atom best?
A) The nucleus occupies very little of the atom's volume, but contains most of its mass.
B) The nucleus occupies a small portion of the atom's volume, and contains little of its mass.
C) The nucleus occupies most of the atom's volume, and contains the majority of its mass.
D) The nucleus occupies the majority of the atom's volume, but contains little of its mass.

2. Which of the following is not a physical change?
A) melting of aspirin
B) lighting a match
C) putting sugar in tea
D) boiling antifreeze

3. The identity of an element is determined by:
A) the number of its protons
B) the number of its electrons
C) its charge
D) its atomic mass

4. An unsaturated solution:
A) hasn't dissolved as much solute as is theoretically possible
B) has dissolved exactly as much solute as is theoretically possible
C) is unstable because it has dissolved more solute than would be expected
D) is heterogeneous

5. A coffee solution is produced when a teaspoon of dry coffee crystals dissolves when mixed in a cup of hot water. The original crystals are classified as a:
A) solute
B) solvent
C) reactant
D) product

Test Your Knowledge: Elements, Compounds, and Mixtures – Answers

1. A
2. B
3. A
4. A
5. A

STATES OF MATTER

The physical states of matter are generally grouped into three main categories:

1. **Solids:** Rigid; they maintain their shape and have strong intermolecular forces.
2. **Liquids:** Cannot maintain their own shape, conform to their containers, and contain forces strong enough to keep molecules from dispersing into spaces.
3. **Gases:** Have indefinite shape; disperse rapidly through space due to random movement and are able to occupy any volume. They are held together by weak forces.

Two specific states of matter are **liquid crystals**, which can maintain their shape as well as be made to flow, and **plasmas**, gases in which electrons are stripped from their nuclei.

There are four physical properties of gases that are related to each other. If any one of these changes, a change will occur in at least one of the remaining three.

1. Volume of the gas.
2. Pressure of the gas.
3. Temperature of the gas.
4. The number of gas molecules.

The laws that relate these properties to each other are:

Boyle's Law: The volume of a given amount of gas at a constant temperature is inversely proportional to pressure. In other words; if the initial volume decreases by half, the pressure will double and vice versa. The representative equation is: $P_1V_1 = P_2V_2$.

Charles's Law: The volume of a given amount of gas at a constant pressure is directly proportional to absolute (Kelvin) temperature. If the temperature of the gas increases, the volume of the gas also increases and vice versa. The representative equation is: $V_1/T_1 = V_2/T_2$.

Avogadro's Law: Equal volumes of all gases under identical conditions of pressure and temperature contain the same number of molecules. The molar volume of all ideal gases at 0° C and a pressure of 1 atm. is 22.4 liters.

The **kinetic theory of gases** assumes that gas molecules are very small compared to the distance between the molecules. Gas molecules are in constant, random motion; they frequently collide with each other and with the walls of whatever container they are in.

Test Your Knowledge: States of Matter

1. Under the same conditions of pressure and temperature, a liquid differs from a gas because the molecules of the liquid:
    a) Have no regular arrangement.
    b) Are in constant motion.
    c) Have stronger forces of attraction between them.
    d) Take the shape of the container they are in.

2. Methane (CH4) gas diffuses through air because the molecules are:
    a) Moving randomly.
    b) Dissolving quickly.
    c) Traveling slowly.
    d) Expanding steadily.

3. Which of the following would not change if the number of gas molecules changed?
    a) Volume of the gas.
    b) Type of gas.
    c) Pressure of the gas.
    d) Temperature of gas.

4. When the pressure is increased on a can filled with gas, its volume ___________.
    a) Stays the same.
    b) Increases.
    c) Decreases.
    d) Turns to liquid.

5. Equal volumes of all gases at the same temperature and pressure contain the same number of molecules. This statement is known as:
    a) Kinetic theory of gases.
    b) Charles's Law.
    c) Boyle's Law.
    d) Avogadro's Law.

Test Your Knowledge: States of Matter – Answers

1. **c)**

2. **a)**

3. **b)**

4. **c)**

5. **d)**

THE PERIODIC TABLE AND CHEMICAL BONDS

The **Periodic Table of Elements** is a chart which arranges the chemical elements in an easy to understand way. Each element is listed in order of increasing atomic number and aligned so that the elements exhibit similar qualities. They are also are arranged in the same row, called a "period," or column often called a "group."

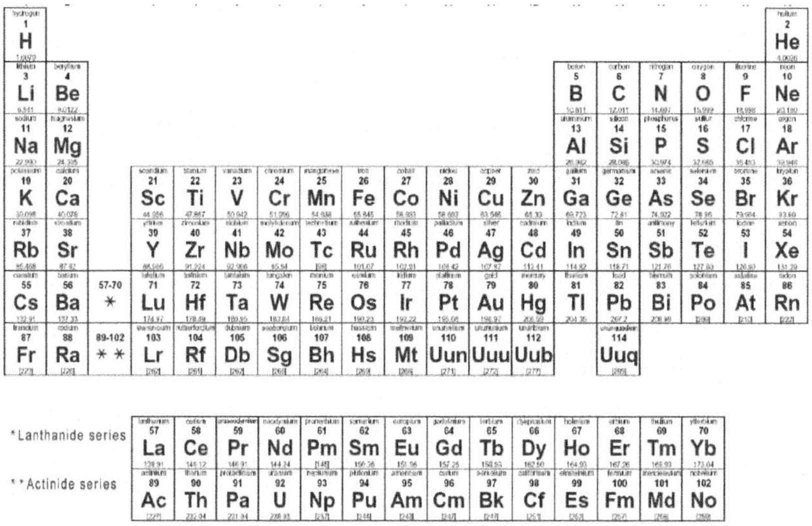

A few other notable trends in the periodic table:

- Every box contains the abbreviated name of the element, its atomic mass, it's atomic number and its atomic weight.
- Elements within a group have the same outer electron arrangement. The number of the main group corresponds to the number of valence electrons in those elements; however, most of the transition elements contain two electrons in their valence shells.
- The horizontal rows correspond to the number of occupied electron shells of the atom.
- The elements set below the main table are the lanthanides (upper row) and actinides. They also usually have two electrons in their outer shells.
- In general, the elements increase in mass from left to right and from top to bottom.

Electronic Structure of Atoms

The electrons of an atom have fixed energy levels called **shells** or principle energy levels. Shells are "filled" with electrons according to specific rules starting with the "inner" shells and working outward. The outermost shell, called the **valance shell**, includes the electrons usually involved in chemical bonding. The octet rule states that atoms of a low atomic number will share, gain, or lose electrons in order to fill the valence shell with eight electrons; this is achieved through different types of bonding. If this shell is full, then the element will be inert.

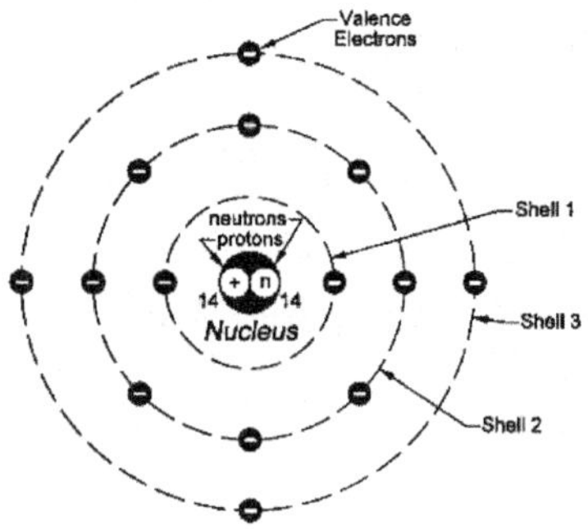

Chemical Bonds

There are three main types of bonds that form between atoms: ionic, covalent, and metallic. In an **ionic bond**, one atom gains electrons to become a negatively charged **anion**, and the other loses electrons to become a positively charged **cations**. The oppositely charged **ions** then bond to each other.

A **covalent bond** forms when atoms share valence electrons. For example, in water, each hydrogen is sharing electrons with the oxygen atom. However, atoms do not always share electrons equally. Atoms that are more **electronegative** will pull electrons toward them more strongly than those that are less electronegative. This difference results in a **polar covalent bond**. A molecule where the electrons are shared equally is **nonpolar**. When atoms share more than one pair of electrons, they form a **double** (two pairs) or **triple** (three pairs) **bond**.

Electrons shared by two metallic atoms create a **metallic bond**. Those electrons participating in metallic bonds may be shared between any of the metal atoms in the region. Most metals have less than four valence electrons, which means they tend to lose electrons and form cations.

VSEPR Bonding Theory

VSEPR (short for Valence Shell Electron Pair Repulsion) **theory** is a method for understanding the three-dimensional structure of covalently-bonded molecules. Because like charges attract, molecules will arrange themselves so that electrons are as far apart as possible. This fact allows us to determine the general shape of many molecules. A few of these are given below.

When there are 3 atoms in a molecule that have no high electronegativity differences, the molecule is **linear**.

Four atoms that have a lone pair on each end result in a **trigonal planar** molecule.

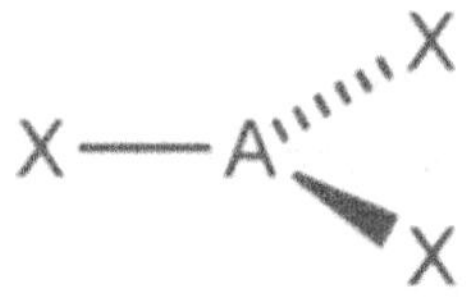

The **tetrahedral** molecule is the standard shape for a single central atom surrounded by four bonds. The bond angles between the different atoms may vary due to differences in electronegativity.

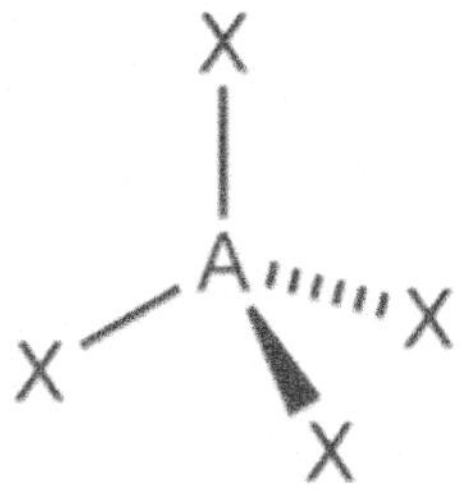

Test Your Knowledge: The Periodic Table and Chemical Bonds

1. What chemical bond forms when anions and cations join together?
A) hydrogen
B) ionic
C) metallic
D) covalence

2. In the periodic table of elements, generally speaking, how do the atomic masses vary?
A) They decrease from left to right and increase from top to bottom.
B) They increase from left to right and increase from bottom to top.
C) They increase from left to right and increase from top to bottom.
D) They increase from right to left and decrease from bottom to top.

3. The force involved in all chemical behavior is:
A) electronegativity
B) covalent bonds
C) electromagnetism
D) ionic bonds

4. Which one of the following is not a type of chemical bond?
A) covalent bond
B) VSEPR bond
C) ionic bond
D) metallic bond

5. Two atoms that do not share electrons equally will form what type of bond?
A) metallic
B) polar covalent
C) ionic
D) hydrogen

Test Your Knowledge: The Periodic Table and Chemical Bonds

1) B
2) C
3) C
4) B
5) B

ACIDS and BASES

There are a number of different technical definitions for acids and bases. In general, an **acid** can be defined as a substance that produces hydrogen ions (H^+) in solution, while a **base** produces hydroxide ions (OH^-). Acidic solutions, which include common liquids like orange juice and vinegar, share a set of distinct characteristics: they have a sour taste and react strongly with metals. Bases, such as bleach and detergents, will taste bitter and have a slippery texture.

The acidity or basicity of a solution is described using its **pH** value, which is the negative log of the concentration of hydrogen ions. A neutral solution, which has the same concentration of hydrogen and hydroxide ions, has a pH of 7. Bases have a pH between 7 and 14, and acids have a pH between 0 and 7. Note that the pH scale is exponential, so a solution with a pH of 2 has one hundred times more hydrogen ions than one with a pH of 4.

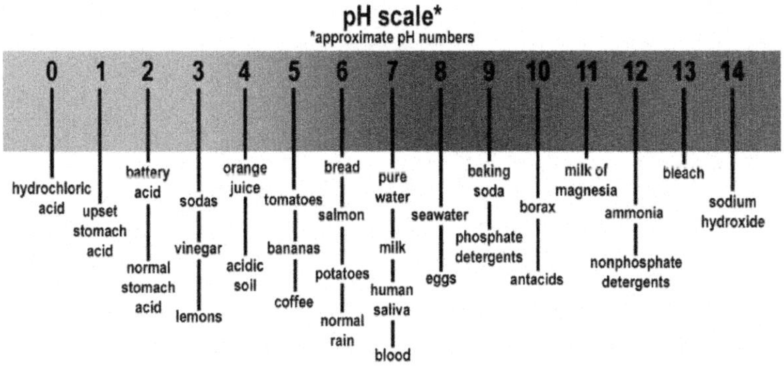

A **buffer** is any solution that exhibits very little change in its pH when small amounts of an acid or base are added to it. An acidic buffer solution is simply one which has a pH less than 7. Often times a weak acid and one of its salts are combined to create an Acidic Buffer. Other times a weak base can be combined with one if its salts to create an Alkaline Buffer. Any solution with a pH greater than 7 would be known as an Alkaline buffer solution.

Most enzymes in the human body only function properly at a precise pH. Our blood has pH of 7.4 which is maintained naturally by our bodies ability to produce a buffer solution. This solution consists of carbonic acid and bicarbonate. If the enzymes lose their precise pH they will often break down no longer be the catalyst of important reactions in the body.

Test Your Knowledge: Acids and Bases

1. One of the characteristic properties of an acid is that it increases the concentration of:
A) hydrogen ions
B) hydroxyl ions
C) hydroxide ions
D) oxide ions

2. A solution with a pH of 12 is:
A) very acidic
B) neutral
C) very basic
D) slightly acidic

4. Proper blood pH level for humans is:
A) 7.0
B) 7.2
C) 7.6
D) 7.4

Test Your Knowledge: Acids and Bases – Answers

1) A
2) C
3) D

Anatomy & Physiology

Anatomy & Physiology is the study of the normal functioning of living organisms and the activities by which life is maintained and transmitted. It includes such things as cell activity, tissues, organs, and processes such as muscle movement, nervous systems, nutrition, digestion, respiration, circulation, and reproduction.

One of the characteristics of living things is that they perform chemical reactions, collectively called metabolism. Cells, the basic units of life, perform many of these metabolic reactions. In a multi-celled organism, cells group together and form tissues that perform the same functions. Tissues group together and form organs and several organs work together in a system.

CELLS, TISSUES, and ORGANS

All organisms are composed of microscopic cells, although the type and number of cells may vary. A cell is the minimum amount of organized living matter that is complex enough to carry out the functions of life. This section will briefly review both animal and plant cells, noting their basic similarities and differences.

Cell Structure

Around the cell is the **cell membrane**, which separates the living cell from the rest of the environment and regulates the comings and goings of molecules within the cell. Because the cell membrane allows some molecules to pass through while blocking others, it is considered **semipermeable.** Each cell's membrane communicates and interacts with the membranes of other cells. In additional to a cell membrane, *plants* also have a **cell wall** which is necessary for structural support and protection. Animal cells do not contain a cell wall.

Organelle

Cells are filled with a gelatin-like substance called **protoplasm** which contains various structures called **organelles**; called so because they act like small versions of organs. The diagram on the next page illustrates the basic organelles of both a plant and an animal cell. Pay attention to the differences and similarities between the two.

PLANT CELL (A)

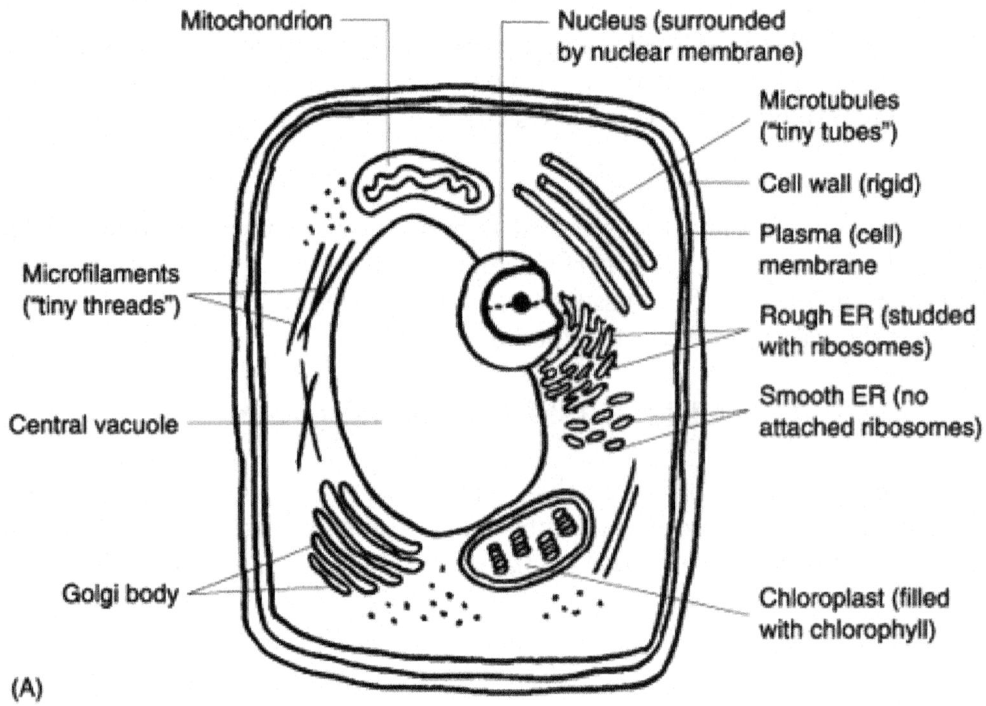

(A)

ANIMAL CELL (B) [2]

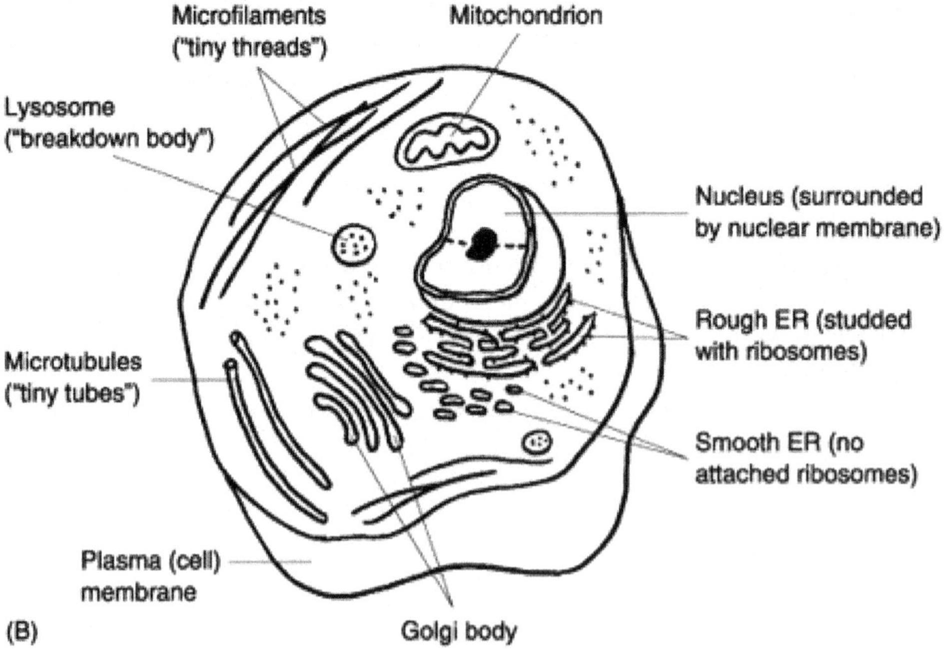

(B)

[2] Graphics from: http://www.education.com

Organelles (Defined)

Mitochondria are spherical or rod-shaped organelles which carry out the reactions of aerobic respiration. They are the power generators of both plant and animal cells, because they convert oxygen and nutrients into ATP, the chemical energy that powers the cell's metabolic activities.

Ribosomes are extremely tiny spheres that make proteins. These proteins are used either as enzymes or as support for other cell functions.

The **Golgi Apparatus** is essential to the production of polysaccharides (carbohydrates), and made up of a layered stack of flattened sacs.

The **Endoplasmic Reticulum** is important in the synthesis and packaging of proteins. It is a complex system of internal membranes, and is called either rough (when ribosomes are attached), or smooth (no ribosomes attached).

Chloroplasts are only found in plants. They contain the chlorophyll molecule necessary for photosynthesis.

The **Nucleus** controls all of the cell's functions, and contains the all-important genetic information, or DNA, of a cell.

Cellular Differentiation

Single-celled organisms have only one cell to carry out all of their required biochemical and structural functions. On the other hand, multi-celled organisms – except for very primitive ones (i.e. sponges) – have various groups of cells called **tissues** that each perform specific functions (**differentiation**).

There are four main types of tissues: **epithelial**, **connective, muscular,** and **nervous**.

Epithelial tissue is made up groups of flattened cells which are grouped tightly together to form a solid surface. Those cells are arranged in one or many layer(s) to form an external or internal covering of the body or organs. Epithelial tissue protects the body from injury and allows for the exchange of gases in the lungs and bronchial tubes. There's even a form of epithelial tissue that produces eggs and sperm, an organism's sex cells.

Connective tissue is made of cells which are surrounded by non-cellular material. For example, bones contain some cells, but they are also surrounded by a considerable amount of non-cellular, extracellular material.

Muscular tissue has the ability to contract. There are three types:

1. **Cardiac** tissue, found in the heart.
2. **Smooth** tissue, located in the walls of hollow internal structures such as blood vessels, the stomach, intestines, and urinary bladder.
3. **Skeletal** (or striated) tissue, found in the muscles.

Nervous tissue consists of cells called **neurons.** Neurons specialize in making many connections with and transmitting electrical impulses to each other. The brain, spinal cord, and peripheral nerves are all made of nervous tissue.

Organs and Organ Systems

As living organisms go through their life cycle, they grow and/or develop. Single-celled organisms grow and develop very rapidly; whereas complex, multi-celled organisms take much longer to progress. All organisms go through changes as they age. These changes involve the development of more complex functions, which in turn require groups of tissues to form larger units called **organs.** Here are some examples of organs:

1. **The Heart**: Made of cardiac muscle and conjunctive tissue (conjunctive tissue makes up the valves), the heart pumps blood first to the lungs in order to pick up oxygen, then through the rest of the body to deliver the oxygen, and finally back to the lungs to start again.

2. **Roots**: A tree's are covered by an epidermis which is in turn made up of a protective tissue. They are also *composed* of tissue, which allows them to grow. The root organ also contains **conductive tissue** to absorb and transport water and nutrients to the rest of the plant.

Generally, in complex organisms like plants and animals, many organs are grouped together into **systems.** For example, many combinations of tissues make up the many organs which create the digestive system in animals. The organs in the digestive system consist of the mouth, the esophagus, the stomach, small and large intestines, the liver, the pancreas, and the gall bladder.

Test Your Knowledge: Cells, Tissues, and Organs

1. Which statement is true about Earth's organisms?
    a) All organisms are based on the cell as the basic unit of life.
    b) Protists are an exception to the cell theory and are not based on cells.
    c) Only single-celled organisms are based on cells.
    d) All organisms are based on tissues as the basic unit of life.

2. What organelle produces the cell's energy source?
    a) Chloroplast.
    b) Nucleus.
    c) Mitochondrion.
    d) Endoplasmic reticulum.

3. The formation of tissue depends upon:
    a) Cell differentiation.
    b) Cell membranes.
    c) Cell death.
    d) Cell organelles.

4. Cardiac muscle is an example of what tissue?
    a) Smooth muscle.
    b) Nervous.
    c) Contractile.
    d) Connective.

5. Which organelle has two forms: rough and smooth?
    a) Mitochondrion.
    b) Golgi apparatus.
    c) Nucleus.
    d) Endoplasmic reticulum.

6. Which organelle is important in the production of polysaccharides (carbohydrates)?
    a) Mitochondrion.
    b) Golgi apparatus.
    c) Nucleus
    d) Endoplasmic reticulum.

Test Your Knowledge: Cells, Tissues, and Organs – Answers

1. **a)**
2. **c)**
3. **a)**
4. **c)**
5. **d)**
6. **b)**

REPRODUCTION

Individual organisms have limited life spans; however, life continues due to reproduction. There are two types of reproduction. One requires the exchange of genetic material between two organisms (**sexual reproduction**), and the other does not (**asexual reproduction**).

Asexual Reproduction

All kingdoms have organisms that engage in asexual reproduction. Asexual reproduction very quickly produces large numbers of genetically identical (or **cloned**) offspring. Some organisms that engage in asexual reproduction can also engage in sexual reproduction at least part of the time.

Comparison Chart

	Asexual Reproduction	**Sexual Reproduction**
Number of organisms involved:	One	Two
Cell division:	Mitosis	Meiosis
Variation in offspring:	No	Yes
Advantages:	Quick. No need to search for mate	Variation
Disadvantages:	No variation	Requires two organisms

In single-celled organisms such as bacteria and protists, asexual reproduction occurs through a process known as **binary fission** (or **bipartition**). The cell first duplicates parts of itself before splitting into two separate, but identical, cells. Some organisms reproduce asexually using the process of **budding**, wherein an offshoot of their body grows into a complete organism.

Many multi-cellular invertebrates can also reproduce asexually by a process called **fragmentation**, where a portion of the organism's body is separated and then grows into a whole organism. This is similar to budding, except that the original body repairs itself as well, leaving behind two complete organisms. Plants can reproduce asexually by budding or fragmentation, when they form tubers, rhizomes, bulbs, and other extensions of their bodies. Plants also have a major sexual phase of their life cycle, which is part of a process called **alternation of generations.**

Alternation of Generations

Although asexual reproduction allows plants to reproduce quickly, most plants engage in sexual reproduction, at least part of the time. Sexually reproducing plants cycle between two distinctly different body types. The first is called the **sporophyte**, and the second is called the **gametophyte.** An adult sporophyte (the part of the plant we see) produces spores. The spores are transported to new areas by animals, wind, water, etc. If the conditions are suitable, those spores will sprout into a **gametophyte** form of the plant, which is not usually seen. This gametophyte produces the eggs and sperm that will join to form a new sporophyte. This change from sporophyte to gametophyte represents an alternation of generations. The gametophyte generation is small and dependent upon the sporophyte generation. An oak tree, for example, is really the sporophyte generation of the plant; the gametophyte generation is contained within its flowers.

Sexual Reproduction

Sexual reproduction is when genetic material from one parent is combined with the genetic material from another, producing offspring that are not identical to either parent. Each parent produces a specialized cell called a **gamete** that contains half of his or her genetic information.

Male animals produce the smaller, more mobile gamete known as a **sperm cell**. Females produce the larger, more sedentary gamete known as an **egg cell**. When these two gametes come into contact, they fuse and combine their genetic information in a process known as **fertilization**. This can happen either externally or internally.

An example of **external fertilization** would be **spawning,** where eggs and sperm are both released into water and must find each other. **Spawning** is dependent upon each gender's reproductive cycle matching the other.

Internal fertilization is dependent upon **copulation**: the process wherein a male deposits sperm cells directly into the reproductive tract of a female. Because a medium like water cannot be used to transport gametes on land, internal fertilization is critical to land-based organisms.

Test Your Knowledge: Reproduction

1. The formation of tubers is an example of what kind of asexual reproduction?
   a) Budding.
   b) Binary fission.
   c) Bipartition.
   d) Root zone development.

2. Which of the following best describes alternation of generation?
   a) The sporophyte produces eggs and sperm that join and lead to the development of a gametophyte.
   b) The gametophyte produces eggs and sperm that join and lead to the development of a sporophyte.
   c) The gametophyte produces eggs and the sporophyte produces sperm that join to form a new plant.
   d) The sporophyte produces eggs and the gametophyte produces sperm that join to form a new plant.

3. In sexually reproducing organisms, gametes come from which parent?
   a) Only the male.
   b) Only the female.
   c) Both the male and female.
   d) Neither.

4. What is the main difference between asexual and sexual reproduction?
   a) Asexual reproduction is only for aquatic organisms.
   b) Asexual reproduction is practiced only by plants.
   c) Humans are the only organisms that utilize sexual reproduction.
   d) Asexual reproduction does not require a mate.

5. Which of the following is **NOT** a form of asexual reproduction?
   a) Fertilization.
   b) Cloning.
   c) Budding.
   d) Fragmentation.

Test Your Knowledge: Reproduction – Answers

1. a)

2. b)

3. c)

4. d)

5. a)

HEREDITY

A duck's webbed feet, a tree whose leaves change color in the fall, and humans having backbones are all characteristics inherited from parent organisms. These inheritable characteristics are transmitted through **genes** and **chromosomes**. In sexual reproduction, each parent contributes half of his or her genes to the offspring.

Genes

Genes influence both what we look like on the outside and how we work on the inside. They contain the information that our bodies need to make the proteins in our bodies. Genes are made of DNA: a double helix (spiral) molecule that consists of two long, twisted strands of nucleic acids. Each of these strands are made of sugar and phosphate molecules, and are connected by pairs of chemicals called **nitrogenous bases** (just bases, for short). There are four types of bases:

1. **Adenine (A).**
2. **Thymine (T).**
3. **Guanine (G).**
4. **Cytosine (C).**

These bases link in a very specific way: **A** always pairs with **T**, and **C** always pairs with **G**.

A gene is a piece of DNA that codes for a specific protein. Each gene contains the information necessary to produce a single trait in an organism, and each gene is different from any other. For example, one gene will code for the protein insulin, and another will code for hair. For any trait, we inherit one gene from our father and one from our mother. Human beings have 20,000 to 25,000 genes, yet those genes only account for about 3% of our DNA.

Alternate forms of the same gene are called **alleles**. When the alleles are identical, the individual is **homozygous** for that trait. When the alleles are different, the individual is **heterozygous** for that trait.

For example, a child may have red hair because she inherited two identical red color genes from each parent; that would make her homozygous for red hair. However, a second child may have brown hair because he inherited different hair color genes from each parent; this would make him heterozygous for brown hair. When genes exist in a heterozygous pairing, usually one is expressed over the other. The gene which is expressed is **dominant**. The unexpressed gene is called **recessive**.

If you took the DNA from all the cells in your body and lined it up, end to end, it would form a (very thin!) strand 6000 million miles long! DNA molecules, and their important genetic material, are tightly packed around proteins called **histones** to make structures called **chromosomes**. Human beings have 23 pairs of chromosomes in every cell, for 46 chromosomes in total. The sex chromosomes determine whether you are a boy (XY) or a girl (XX). The other chromosomes are called autosomes.

Patterns of Inheritance

Biologists refer to the genetic makeup of an organism as its **genotype**. However, the collection of physical characteristics that result from the action of genes is called an organism's **phenotype.** You can remember this differentiation by looking at the beginning of each word: *geno*type is *gen*etic, and *pheno*type is *phy*sical. Patterns of inheritance can produce surprising results, because the genotype determines the phenotype.

Test Your Knowledge: Heredity

1. On paired chromosomes, two identical alleles are called:
    a) Heterozygous.
    b) Homozygous.
    c) Tetrad.
    d) Binomial.

2. The physical characteristics of an organism are known as its:
    a) Chromosomes.
    b) Genotype.
    c) DNA.
    d) Phenotype.

3. Which of the following is **NOT** a nucleotide found in DNA?
    a) Uracil.
    b) Guanine.
    c) Cytosine.
    d) Thymine.

4. The genotype describes an organism's:
    a) Appearance.
    b) Genetic code.
    c) Type of DNA.
    d) Eye color only.

5. The shape of the DNA molecule is a:
    a) Single spiral.
    b) Double spiral.
    c) Straight chain.
    d) Bent chain.

Test Your Knowledge: Heredity – Answers

1. **b)**

2. **d)**

3. **a)**

4. **b)**

5. **b)**

THE RESPIRATORY SYSTEM

The human respiratory system is made up of a series of organs responsible for taking in oxygen and expelling carbon dioxide, and can be divided into two parts: **air conduction** and **gas exchange.** (We'll cover those in more detail soon.)

The respiratory system's primary organs are the lungs, which take in oxygen and expel carbon dioxide when we breathe. Breathing involves **inhalation** (the taking in of air) and **exhalation** (the releasing of air). Blood gathers oxygen from the lungs and transports it to cells throughout the body, where it exchanges the oxygen for carbon dioxide. The carbon dioxide is then transported back to the lungs, where it is exhaled.

Air Conduction

The **diaphragm**, a dome-shaped muscle located at the bottom of the lungs, controls breathing. When a breath is taken, the diaphragm flattens and pulls forward, making more space for the lungs. During exhalation, the diaphragm expands upwards to force air out.

Humans breathe through their noses or mouths, which causes air to enter the **pharynx (**upper part of the throat). The air then passes the **larynx** (the Adam's apple on the inside of the throat). The larynx is also known as the voice box because it changes shape to form sounds. Inhaled air passes into a tube in the center of the chest known as the **trachea**, (the windpipe) which filters the air.

The trachea branches into two **bronchi**, two tubes which carry air into the lungs. Once inside the lungs, each bronchus branches into smaller tubes called **bronchioles**. Bronchioles then lead to sac-like structures called **alveoli**, where the second function of the respiratory system – gas exchange – occurs.

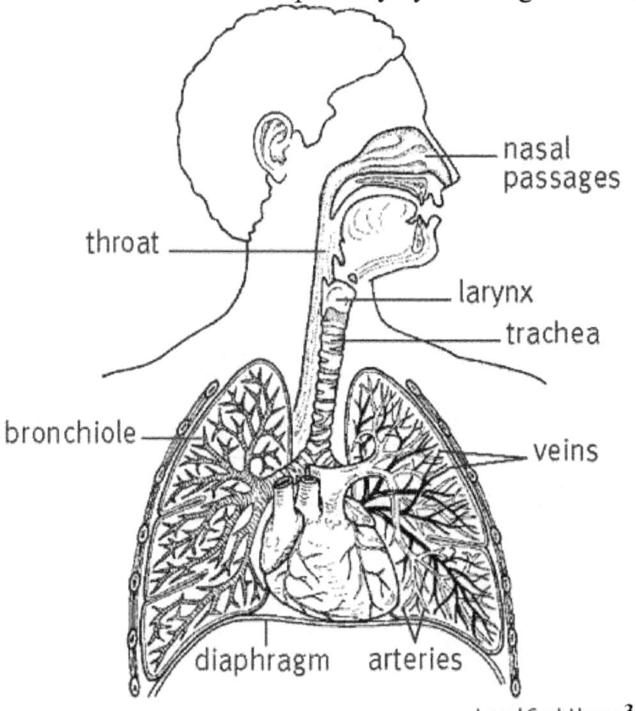

Laurel Cook Lhowe [3]

Gas Exchange

[3] The American Heritage® Science Dictionary Copyright © 2010 by Houghton Mifflin Harcourt Publishing Company. Published by Houghton Mifflin Harcourt Publishing Company.

Each lung contains over two million alveoli, which creates a large surface area for gas exchange: approximately 800 square feet!

The alveoli and the surrounding blood vessels have very thin walls, which allows for the diffusion of gases in either direction – specifically oxygen and carbon dioxide. Air entering the lungs from the atmosphere is high in oxygen and low in carbon dioxide. This means that the alveoli have a high concentration of oxygen and a low concentration of carbon dioxide.

The opposite is true for the blood within the alveoli's blood vessels. Blood entering the lungs is *low* in oxygen and *high* in carbon dioxide because of cellular respiration (metabolism).

Because the alveoli have a high concentration of oxygen and a low concentration of carbon dioxide, while their blood vessels have the opposite condition, the two gases flow in opposite directions (gas exchange).

Plants exchange gas as well. Single-celled plants, like their animal counterparts, simply exchange gases through the cell membranes. Multicellular plants use pores on the leaf surface, called **stomata**, to exchange gases with the atmosphere.

Test Your Knowledge: The Respiratory System

1. The conduction of air through the respiratory system follows which of the following paths?
    a) Pharynx, larynx, alveoli, trachea, bronchus, bronchioles.
    b) Alveoli, bronchioles, bronchus, trachea, larynx, pharynx.
    c) Pharynx, larynx, trachea, bronchus, bronchioles, alveoli.
    d) Bronchus, bronchioles, alveoli, pharynx, larynx, trachea.

2. Each alveolus in the lungs is covered by tiny blood vessels to perform which of these functions?
    a) Excretion of fluids.
    b) Gas exchange.
    c) Blood production.
    d) Air intake.

3. The pores on a plant leaf that allow for gas exchange are called:
    a) Alveoli.
    b) Cell pores.
    c) Membrane gaps.
    d) Stomata.

4. Which of the following occurs during gas exchange in a cell?
    a) Oxygen is flowing from a low concentration inside the cell to a high concentration outside the cell.
    b) Oxygen is flowing from a high concentration in the red blood cells to a low concentration inside the body cell.
    c) Carbon dioxide is moving from the red blood cells into the body cells, while oxygen is moving from the body cells into the red blood cells.
    d) Carbon dioxide is flowing from a low concentration outside the cells to a high concentration inside the cells.

5. The lungs are very efficient at gas exchange because they have a:
    a) High mass.
    b) Low volume.
    c) High surface-area-to-volume ratio.
    d) Low surface-area-to-volume ratio.

Test Your Knowledge: The Respiratory System – Answers

1. **c)**

2. **b)**

3. **d)**

4. **b)**

5. **c)**

THE SKELETAL SYSTEM

Skeletal systems provide structure, support, form, protection, and movement. Of course, muscles do the actual *moving* of an organism, but bones – a major component of the skeletal system –create the framework through which muscles and organs connect. The bone marrow in animal skeletal systems performs **hematopoiesis** (the manufacturing of both red blood cells and white blood cells).

Skeletal systems come in many different forms - those inside of the body are called **endoskeletons**, while those skeletal structures formed outside of the body are known as **exoskeletons**. Crabs and insects have hard shells made of **chitin** to protect their entire bodies. Some organisms, such as starfish, have skeletons made up of tubes filled with fluids running through their bodies. These fluid skeletal systems are called **hydrostatic**.

Joints are where two bones come together. **Connective tissues** at the joint prevent the bones from damaging each other. Joints can be freely movable (elbow or knee), slightly movable (vertebrae in the back), or immovable (skull).

Plants also have a need for support, shape, and protection. While nonvascular do not have a great need for support (remember, they don't grow very tall), vascular plants require a great deal of support. Remember cell walls (a semi-permeable, rigid structure that surrounds each cell outside the cell membrane)? The support and structure of plant cells are primarily derived from the cell wall. Additional support and structure is provided by the tubes used to move water and nutrients through the plant.

Test Your Knowledge: The Skeletal System

1. Which of the following is NOT a function of the skeletal system in animals?
   a) Transport fluids.
   b) Produce oil.
   c) Placement of internal organs.
   d) Production of blood cells.

2. Which of the following is true of bones?
   a) They contain nerves.
   b) Some are unbreakable.
   c) They are present in vertebrates.
   d) They directly touch each other at a joint.

3. Which of the following animals does **NOT** have an exoskeleton?
   a) Insects.
   b) Crabs.
   c) Lobsters.
   d) Earthworms.

4. What type of tissue is found at joints and protects bones from rubbing against each other and becoming damaged?
   a) Contractile.
   b) Connective.
   c) Conductive.
   d) Catabolic.

5. Fluid skeletal systems are _______________.
   a) Hydrostatic.
   b) Hydrolic.
   c) Hydrophobic.
   d) Hydroskeleton.

Test Your Knowledge: The Skeletal System – Answers

1. b)

2. c)

3. d)

4. b)

5. a)

THE DIGESTIVE SYSTEM

The **digestive system** is a system of organs in the body that is responsible for the intake and processing of food and the removal of food waste products. The digestive system ensures that the body has the necessary nutrients and the energy it needs to function.

The digestive system includes the **gastrointestinal** (GI) **tract**, which is formed by the organs through which the food passes on its way through the body:

1. oral cavity

2. pharynx

3. esophagus

4. stomach

5. small intestines

6. large intestines

Throughout the digestive system there are also organs that have a role in processing food Even though food doesn't pass through them directly. These include the teeth, tongue, salivary glands, liver, gallbladder, and pancreas.

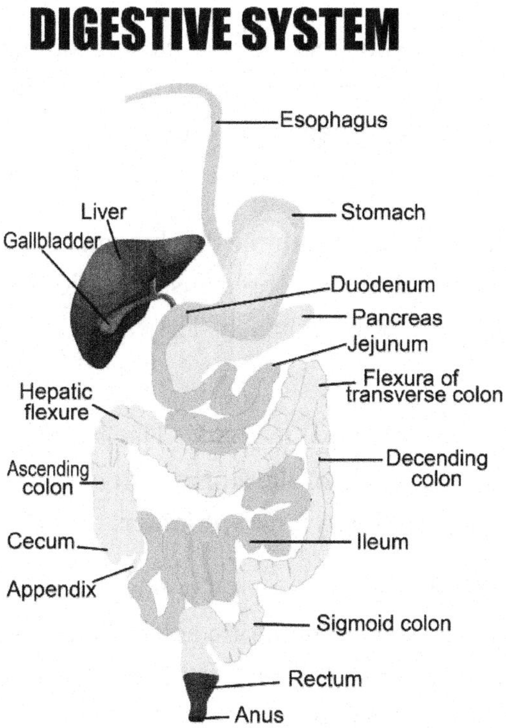

The Mouth

The digestive system begins with the **mouth**. Also known as the oral cavity, the mouth contains other organs that play a role in digestion. The **teeth** are small organs that cut and grind food. They are located on the edges of the mouth, are made out of dentin, which is a substance that resembles bone, and are covered by enamel. The teeth are very hard organs, and each of them has its own blood vessels and nerves, which are located in the matter that fills the tooth, called the pulp.

Also in the mouth is the **tongue**, which is a muscle located behind the teeth. The tongue contains the taste buds and moves food around the mouth as it's being processed by the teeth. It then moves food towards the pharynx when it's time to swallow. The **salivary glands**, located around the mouth, produce saliva. There are three pairs of salivary glands, and the saliva they produce lubricates and digests carbohydrates.

The Pharynx

The **pharynx** is a tube that enables the passage of food and air further into the body. This structure performs two functions. The pharynx needs the help of the epiglottis, which allows food to pass to the esophagus by covering the opening of the larynx, a structure that carries air into the lungs. When you need to breathe in, the esophagus is closed, so the air passes only into the larynx.

The Esophagus

The **esophagus** begins at the pharynx and continues to carry food all the way to the stomach. The esophagus is a muscular tube, and the muscles in its wall help to push food down. During vomiting, it pushes food up.

The esophagus has two rings of muscle, called **sphincters**. These sphincters close at the top and the bottom ends of the esophagus when food is not passing through it. Heartburn occurs when the bottom sphincter cannot close entirely and allows the contents of the stomach to enter the esophagus.

The Stomach

The stomach is a round organ located on the left side of the body just beneath the diaphragm. It is divided into four different regions. The **cardia** connects the stomach to the esophagus, transitioning from the tube-like shape of the esophagus into the sack shape of the rest of the stomach. The cardia is also where the lower sphincter of the esophagus is located.

The **body** of the stomach is its largest part, and the **fundus** is located above the body. The last part of the stomach is the **pylorus**, a funnel shaped region located beneath the body of the stomach. It controls the passage of partially digested food further down the GI tract through the **pyloric sphincter**.

The stomach is made out of four layers of tissue. The innermost layer, the **mucosa**, contains a smooth muscle and the mucus membrane that secretes digestive enzymes and hydrochloric acid. The cells that secrete these products are located within the small pores called the **gastric pits**. The mucus membrane also secretes mucus to protect the stomach from its own digestive enzymes.

The **submucosa** is located around the mucosa and is made of connective tissue; it contains nerves and the blood vessels. The **muscularis** layer enables the movement of the stomach; it's made up of three layers of smooth muscle. This layer enables the movement of the stomach. The outermost layer of the stomach is the serosa. It secretes **serous fluid** that keeps the stomach wet and reduces friction between the stomach and the surrounding organs.

The Small Intestine

The **small intestine** continues from the stomach and takes up most of the space in the abdomen. It's attached to the wall of the abdomen and measures around twenty-two feet long.

The small intestine can be divided into three parts. The **duodenum** is the part of the small intestine that receives the food and chemicals from the stomach. The **jejunum**, which continues from the duodenum, is where most of the nutrients are absorbed into the blood. Lastly, the **ileum**, which continues from the jejunum, is where the rest of the nutrients are absorbed.

Absorption in the small intestine is helped by the **villi**, which are small protrusions that increase the surface area available for absorption. The villi are made out of smaller microvilli.

The Liver and Gallbladder

The **liver** is not a part of the GI tract. However, it performs roles that are vital for digestion and life itself. The liver is located just beneath the diaphragm and is the largest organ in the body after the skin. It's triangular in shape, and extends across the whole width of the abdomen.

The liver is divided into four lobes: the left lobe, the right lobe, the caudate lobe (which wraps around the inferior vena cava), and the quadrate lobe (which wraps around the gallbladder). The liver is connected to the peritoneum by the coronary, left, right, and falciform ligaments.

The liver is responsible for a number of functions, including detoxification of the blood, storage of nutrients, and production of components of blood plasma. Its role in digestion is to produce **bile**, a fluid that aids in the digestion of fats. After its production, bile is carried through the bile ducts to the **gallbladder**, a small muscular pear-shaped organ that stores and releases bile.

The Pancreas

The **pancreas** is another organ that is not part of the GI tract but which plays a role in digestion. It's located below and to the left of the stomach. The pancreas secretes both the enzymes that digest food and the hormones insulin and glucagon, which control blood sugar levels.

The pancreas is what is known as a **heterocrine gland**, which means it contains both endocrine tissue, which produces insulin and glucagon that move directly into the bloodstream, and exocrine tissue, which produces digestive enzymes that pass into the small intestine. These enzymes include:

- pancreatic amylase: breaks large polysaccharides into smaller sugars
- trypsin, chymotrypsin, and carboxypeptidase: break down proteins into amino acid subunits
- pancreatic lipase: breaks down large fat molecules into fatty acids and monoglyceride
- ribonuclease and deoxyribonuclease: digest nucleic acids.

The Large Intestine

The **large intestine** continues from the small intestine and loops around it. No digestion actually takes part in the large intestine. Rather, it absorbs water and some leftover vitamins. The large intestine carries waste (feces) to the **rectum**, where it's stored until it's expelled through the **anus**.

Test Your Knowledge: The Digestive System

1. Food passes through all of the following organs except:
A) stomach
B) large intestine
C) esophagus
D) liver

2. How many pair(s) of salivary glands are in the human body?
A) 1
B) 2
C) 3
D) 4

3. The esophagus performs all of the following functions except:
A) connecting the pharynx to the stomach
B) preventing stomach acid from reaching the pharynx
C) pushing food into the stomach
D) moving food from the stomach to the small intestine

4. Which layer of the stomach contains blood vessels and nerves?
A) the mucosa
B) the submucosa
C) the serosa
D) the cardia

5. Bile is stored in the
A) liver
B) duodenum
C) gallbladder
D) pancreas

Test Your Knowledge: The Digestive System – Answers

1) D
2) C
3) D
4) B
5) C

THE MUSCULAR SYSTEM

Muscles are often viewed as the "machines" of the body. They help move food from one organ to another, and carry out physical movement. There are three types of muscles in our body: cardiac, smooth, and skeletal. The nervous system controls all three types of muscle tissue, both consciously (controlled) and unconsciously (automatic).

Skeletal (or **striated**) muscle tissue is consciously controlled. The muscle is attached to bones, and when it contracts, the bones move. Skeletal tissue also forms visible muscles, as well as much of the body mass.

Smooth muscle is under automatic control and is generally found in the internal organs, especially in the intestinal tract and in the walls of blood vessels.

Cardiac muscle is found only in the heart. This type of muscle tissue is so automated that it will continue to contract even without stimulation from the nervous system. Isolated heart cells in a dish will continue to contract on their own until oxygen or nutrient sources are used up.

Muscle contraction begins when a nerve impulse causes the release of a chemical called a **neurotransmitter**. Muscle contraction is explained as the interaction between two necessary muscle proteins: thick bands of **myosin** and thin bands of a**ctin**. The thick myosin filaments have small knob-like projections that grab onto the thin actin filaments. As these knobs move slightly, they pull the actin filaments, which slide alongside the myosin filaments. This has the effect of shortening the muscle and thus causing a contraction.

Connective tissues known as **tendons** form a link between muscles and bones (whereas **ligaments** form a link between two bones). The contraction of a muscle causes an exertion of force upon the tendon, which then pulls its attached bone. This movement is synchronized by the central nervous system and results in movement.

Uni-cellular organisms, such as protists and sperm cells, have the ability to move as well. This kind of movement can be accomplished in three different ways. In the case of amoebas, which are one-celled formless blobs of protoplasm, movement is accomplished by extending a portion of the cell itself and then flowing into that portion. Other organisms use **cilia,** which are tiny hair-like projections from the cell membrane, or **flagellum**, which is a tail-like projection that whips around or spins to move.

Test Your Knowledge: The Muscular System

1. What are the three types of muscle cells?
    a) Cardiac, synaptic, and skeletal.
    b) Cardiac, autonomic, and smooth.
    c) Skeletal, cardiac, and smooth.
    d) Smooth, cardiac, and spinal.

2. Which of the following is true about skeletal muscles?
    a) They all contract unconsciously.
    b) All muscle movement is consciously controlled.
    c) They connect directly to one another.
    d) They are also known as striated muscles.

3. What two protein molecules are needed for muscles to contract?
    a) Pepsin and insulin.
    b) Myosin and pepsin.
    c) Hemoglobin and insulin.
    d) Myosin and actin.

4. Flagellum and cilia:
    a) Work with an organism's muscles for movement.
    b) Are parts of all cells and are required for movement.
    c) Are used by organisms without muscular systems.
    d) None of the above.

5. Peristalsis is a process performed by which type of muscle tissue?
    a) Catabolic.
    b) Cardiac.
    c) Smooth.
    d) Skeletal.

Test Your Knowledge: The Muscular System – Answers

1. **c)**

2. **d)**

3. **d)**

4. **c)**

5. **c)**

THE CIRCULATORY SYSTEM (CARDIOVASCULAR SYSTEM)

The cells in living organisms need to receive nutrients and have their waste products removed. Single-celled organisms are able to pass these substances to and from their environment directly through the cell membrane. However, in multi-celled organisms, these substances are transported by way of the circulatory system.

The cardiovascular system has three main parts: the heart (which is the pump in the system), the blood vessels providing a route for fluids in the system, and the blood which transports nutrients and oxygen and contains waste products.

Heart

The human heart has four chambers – right atrium, right ventricle, left atrium, and left ventricle – which separate fresh blood from the blood that is full of cellular waste.

When leaving the heart, blood travels through **arteries**. To remember this, imagine that the "a" in "arteries" stands for "away". *A*rteries carry blood *a*way from the heart. On its way to the heart, blood travels through **veins.**

The **superior vena cava** is the vein which brings blood from the body into the top right chamber of the heart. This top right chamber is called the **right atrium**. The right atrium is separated from the chamber below it by a valve, and separated from the chamber next to it by a wall of muscle tissue. The heart relaxes after each beat, which allows blood to flow from the right atrium, through the valve, and into the chamber below called the **right ventricle.**

The right ventricle sends blood through the **pulmonary arteries** to the lungs. Blood picks up oxygen in the lungs and then is moved through the **pulmonary veins** back to the upper part of the heart. But this time, it enters on the left side into the **left atrium.** Use that first-letter rule again to remember this: blood from the *l*ungs enters the *l*eft atrium.

The left atrium – like the right – is separated from the left ventricle below it by a valve. When this valve opens during the relaxed phase of the heart, blood flows into the left ventricle. This chamber has the largest and strongest muscular wall so that it can force blood into the **aorta**, which is the body's largest artery, pulling blood away from the heart to the rest of the body.

The Heart:

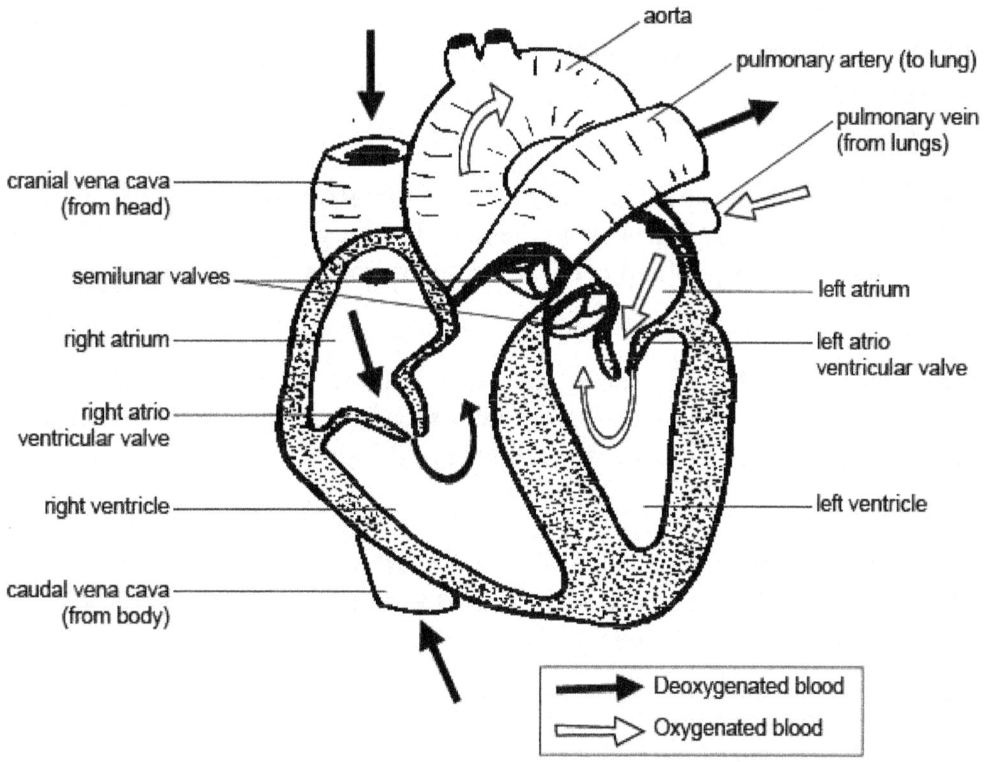

[4]

Arteries branch off from the aorta and travel to all parts of the body, continuing to branch and get smaller until they become **arterioles.** Arterioles lead to very small beds of tiny blood vessels called **capillaries.** Capillary beds are the site where the exchange of nutrients, gases, and wastes occurs. Blood that now contains wastes leaves the capillary beds, and enters small vessels called **venules**. These travel back through the body to the heart, becoming larger veins on the way, ending with the **large vena cava vein** that empties into the heart.

This begins the cycle all over again!

Things the Circulatory System Carries:

- Oxygen from the lungs to the body's cells.
- Carbon dioxide from the body's cells to the lungs.
- Nutrients from the digestive system to the cells.
- Waste products, other than carbon dioxide, to the liver and kidneys.
- Hormones and other messenger chemicals, from the glands and organs of their production to the body's cells.

---

[4] Graphic from: http://www.en.wikibooks.org

Blood

Blood helps regulate our internal environment and keeps us in a generally constant state known as **homeostasis**. Blood transports and mixes elements up, making it possible for all the organs to contribute to maintaining homeostasis.

Blood is not a liquid; it is a **suspension** (fluids containing particles suspended inside them). Blood has two components: **plasma**, the liquid part, and the solid **blood cells** suspended throughout. There are three major types of cells: **red blood cells**, **white blood cells**, and cellular fragments called **platelets.**

Plasma

Plasma is mostly water, in which some substances such as proteins, hormones, and nutrients (glucose sugar, vitamins, amino acids, and fats) are dissolved. Gases (carbon dioxide and oxygen), salts (of calcium, chloride, and potassium), and wastes other than carbon dioxide are also dissolved in blood.

Red Blood Cells

Red blood cells contain a protein molecule called **hemoglobin**, which holds an atom of iron. The hemoglobin molecule binds with oxygen and carbon dioxide, thus providing the mechanism by which the red blood cells can carry these gases around the body.

White Blood Cells

White blood cells come in many specialized forms and are used in the immune system to fight off invading organisms and keep us from getting diseases.

Platelets

Platelets release substances at the site of a wound that start the blood-clotting reaction.

Circulation within Plants

In plants, the transport system is based on the special properties of water.

The cells that make up the vascular tissue of plants form a continuous system of tubes running from the roots, through the stems, and to the leaves. Water and nutrients flow to the leaves through a vascular tissue called **xylem**, where they are used in the process of photosynthesis. Following that process, the products of photosynthesis then flow through a vascular tissue called **phloem** back down to the roots.

Test Your Knowledge: The Circulatory System

1. Which of the following is NOT one of the chambers in the four-chambered vertebrate heart?
   a) Right atrium.
   b) Right ventricle.
   c) Left alveolar.
   d) Left ventricle.

2. Which of the following is true about blood flow in the four-chambered vertebrate heart circulatory system?
   a) Blood in the pulmonary vein is oxygenated.
   b) Blood in the pulmonary artery is oxygenated.
   c) Blood in the aorta is not oxygenated.
   d) Blood in the vena cava is oxygenated.

3. Which of the following are the major components of blood?
   a) Proteins and lipids.
   b) Plasma and cells.
   c) Proteins and platelets.
   d) Dells and lipids.

4. Platelets perform which of the following functions?
   a) Blood clotting.
   b) Carrying oxygen.
   c) Carrying carbon dioxide.
   d) Disease protection.

5. Capillary beds occur between:
   a) Arteries and veins.
   b) Aortas and vena cavas.
   c) Arterioles and venules.
   d) Atria and ventricles.

6. Red blood cells perform which of the following functions?
   a) Blood clotting.
   b) Carrying oxygen and carbon dioxide.
   c) Disease protection.
   d) Wound healing.

7. Xylem and phloem are plant tissues that:
   a) Produce sugar molecules and oxygen.
   b) Transport water and nutrients throughout the plant.
   c) Contain chloroplasts.
   d) Produce seeds.

8. The products of photosynthesis in the leaves flow to the roots through vascular tissue called:
   a) Phloem.
   b) Xylem.
   c) Meristem.
   d) Angiosperm.

Test Your Knowledge: The Circulatory System – Answers

1. **c)**
2. **a)**
3. **b)**
4. **a)**
5. **c)**
6. **b)**
7. **b)**
8. **a)**

THE RENAL SYSTEM (FILTRATION/EXCRETION SYSTEM)

Single-celled organisms excrete toxic substances either by diffusion through their cell membranes, or through specialized organelles called **vacuoles.** When metabolic chemical reactions occur within the cells of organisms, wastes are produced that could cause harm to the body. Those wastes therefore must be excreted. Multicellular organisms require special organ systems – humans specifically utilize the circulatory and excretory systems – to eliminate wastes.

Organisms need to be able to respond to changes in their external environment, all the while still maintaining a relatively constant internal environment. They must maintain a balance of water, temperature, and salt concentration, to name just a few. The physical and chemical processes that work to maintain an internal balance are called **homeostasis.** You may recognize this term from the previous discussion on blood and the circulatory system. Homeostasis is maintained by the cooperation of both the circulatory and the renal systems.

We have discussed digestions: food is broken down, absorbed as very small molecules, and carried to the cells by blood. Cells need these broken-down molecules to perform the life-sustaining biochemical reactions of metabolism, which produce wastes.

1. Aerobic respiration produces water and **carbon dioxide**.
2. Anaerobic respiration produces **lactic acid** and carbon dioxide.
3. Dehydration synthesis produces water.
4. Protein metabolism produces **nitrogenous wastes**, (i.e. **ammonia**).
5. Other metabolic processes can produce salts, oils, etc.

Non-toxic wastes can be retained, released, or recycled through other reactions. **Toxic** wastes however, are disposed of according to their molecular make-up. For example, blood carries gaseous wastes like carbon dioxide to the lungs for exhalation. Other wastes need to be filtered out of the blood and then excreted. Nitrogenous wastes are the result of excess amino acids broken down during cellular respiration. The toxicity (harmfulness) of those nitrogenous wastes varies from:

Extremely Toxic - **Ammonia**
Less Toxic - **Urea**
Non-toxic – **Uric Acid**

The Kidneys

Toxic wastes are carried by blood to the liver, where they are converted into **urea.** The blood then carries the urea to the **kidneys** (bean-shaped, fist-sized organs), where it will be converted from urea into **urine**. Urine is able to mix with water and be excreted from the body; the amount of water that is used in this process is regulated by the kidneys in order to prevent body dehydration.

The kidneys are complex filtering systems which maintain the proper levels of various life-supporting substances, including sodium; potassium; chloride; calcium; glucose sugar; and amino acids. These life-supporting substances are absorbed by the kidneys from urine before it I expelled. The kidneys also help maintain blood pressure and the acidity (pH) level of the blood.

Each kidney contains at least a million individual units called **nephrons.** Nephrons perform similar functions as the alveoli do in the lungs; but whereas the alveoli function as areas of gas exchange, the kidney nephrons are structured to function as areas of *fluid* interchange. Each nephron contains a bed of capillaries. Those capillaries which are bringing in blood are surrounded by a **Bowman's capsule**.

A Bowman's capsule is an important part of the filtration system in the kidneys. The capsule separates the blood into two components: a cleaned blood product, and a filtrate which is moved through the nephron. As the filtrate travels through the nephron, more impurities are removed. The filtrate is concentrated into **urine**, which is then processed for elimination. The collected urine flows into the **ureters**, which take it to the **urinary bladder**. Urine will collect in the urinary bladder until the pressure causes an urge to expel it from the body through the **urethra**.

Each nephron in the kidneys is attached to its own Bowman's capsule, and there are hundreds of thousands of nephrons. Functioning kidneys can process the blood in the body about 20 times each day, illustrating just how important these structures are. The kidneys are truly a feat of natural engineering. In fact, despite the medical community's best efforts, it has so far been impossible to build a fully artificial kidney.

Kidneys also regulate the amount of water circulating in the bloodstream. If the brain detects depleted levels of water in the blood, it increases the release of the **antidiuretic hormone** (**ADH**). ADH causes the kidneys to reabsorb water into the bloodstream, which in turn concentrates the urine and preserves water for the body. The reason why you urinate more frequently when drinking alcohol is because alcohol inhibits the ADH signal from the brain.

Test Your Knowledge: The Renal System

1. The kidneys filter which of the following from blood?
    a) Undigested food.
    b) Metabolic wastes.
    c) Blood cells.
    d) Platelets.

2. Which of the following is **NOT** a function of the kidneys?
    a) Regulating pH (acidity) of blood.
    b) Regulating blood pressure.
    c) Assisting in the maintenance of homeostasis.
    d) Regulating hormone release.

3. The nephron is where ____________ is produced.
    a) Urine.
    b) Ammonia.
    c) Nucleic acid.
    d) Amino acid.

4. Waste concentrated in the Bowman's capsule is called:
    a) Urine.
    b) Salts.
    c) Nucleic acids.
    d) Amino acids.

5. Alcohol consumption increases urination because it:
    a) Increases the amount of water in the body.
    b) Increases the action of antidiuretic hormone.
    c) Decreases the action of antidiuretic hormone.
    d) Stops water reabsorption.

Test Your Knowledge: The Renal System – Answers

1. **b)**

2. **d)**

3. **a)**

4. **a)**

5. **c)**

THE NERVOUS SYSTEM

Irritability is a term used to describe an organism's response to changes, or **stimuli**, in its surroundings. All living organisms respond to environmental stimulus, usually by taking some sort of action: movement of a muscle, gland secretion, activating entire systems like digestion, etc.

Plants have cellular receptors that use chemical messengers to detect and respond to aspects of their environment such as light, gravity, and touch. For example, the orientation of a plant toward or away from light, called **phototropism** is mediated by hormones.

In multi-celled animals, a nervous system controls these responses.

The functioning unit of the nervous system is the **neuron**, a cell with structures capable of transmitting electrical impulses. A neuron must be able to first receive information from internal or external sources, before integrating the signal and sending it to another neuron, gland, or muscle. In multi-celled vertebrates, each neuron has four regions.

At one end of the neuron, there are branch-like extensions called **dendrites**, which receive signals from other neurons.

The **cell body** of the neuron is where the cellular functions take place and where signals are integrated.

The **axon** is an extension from the cell body which the nerve impulses travel along. Axons can be several feet in length, carrying signals from one end of the body to the other.

At the very end of the axon is the **synaptic terminal**, an area that contains chemical substances called **neurotransmitters.**

When an electrical nerve signal reaches the synaptic terminal, it causes neurotransmitters to be released. Neurotransmitters then move across the small space between the neuron and the next neuron (or gland or muscle). This small space is called the **synapse.** Once across the synapse, the neurotransmitter is received by the dendrites of another neuron (or the receptors on a gland or muscle) and then turned back into an electrical signal to be passed on.

The nervous system is divided into two main systems, the **central nervous system** (**CNS**) and the **peripheral nervous system** (PNS).

CNS

The central nervous system consists of the brain and spinal cord (contained within the vertebral column or backbone). The brain integrates all the signals in the nervous system, and therefore is responsible for controlling every aspect of the body.

PNS

The peripheral nervous system consists of the nerves outside of the brain and spinal cord. The main function of the PNS is to connect the CNS to the limbs, organs, and **senses**. Unlike the CNS, the PNS is not protected by the bone of spine and skull. This leaves the PNS exposed to toxins and mechanical injuries.

The peripheral nervous system is divided into the **somatic nervous system** and the **autonomic nervous system**.

The **somatic nervous system** deals with motor functions. Its nerves connect with skeletal muscle and control movement of all kinds, from fine motor skills to walking and running.

The **autonomic nervous system** works mostly without our conscious control. It is often responsible for critical life functions such as breathing and heart rate. The autonomic nervous system has two divisions.

The **sympathetic division** is responsible for the fight-or-flight response; it prepares the body for high-energy, stressful situations.

The **parasympathetic division** is responsible for rest and digestion functions, so it tends to slow down the body.

Nerves from each of these divisions usually make contact with the same organs, but they often have opposite effects.

The Endocrine System

Another important system in our body is the endocrine, or glandular, system. It controls growth rate, feelings of hunger, body temperature, and more. Many organs run the endocrine system: the **pituitary gland**, the **pancreas**, the **ovaries** (only in females) and **testes** (only in males), the **thyroid** gland, the **parathyroid** gland, the **adrenal** glands, etc.

Of all these, the pituitary gland is the most important endocrine gland in your body. About the size of a pea, the pituitary gland hangs down from the base of your brain and produces the hormone which controls growth.

Fun Fact: Humans grow faster at night because more hormones are released into your blood when you are sleeping.

Test Your Knowledge: The Nervous System

1. __________ is the functional unit of the nervous system.

a) The nephron
b) The nucleus
c) The neuron
d) The neutrophil

2. Which of the following is a part of the CNS?

a) Autonomic nerves.
b) Sympathetic nerves.
c) Peripheral nerves.
d) Spinal cord nerves.

3. Dendrites receive information from:

a) The axon of other neurons.
b) The dendrites of other neurons.
c) The cell body of other neurons.
d) The nucleus of other neurons.

4. __________ release neurotransmitters (the chemical substance that carries messages between cells).

a) Axons.
b) Dendrites.
c) Cell bodies.
d) The nucleus.

5. Which of the following is NOT true about irritability?

a) Plants do not experience irritability.
b) Activates neurons in the brain.
c) Requires axons in animals.
d) Neurons act upon muscles.

Test Your Knowledge: The Nervous System – Answers

1. **c)**
2. **d)**
3. **a)**
4. **a)**
5. **a)**

Physics

Physics is the science of matter and energy, and of interactions between the two, grouped in traditional fields such as acoustics, optics, mechanics, thermodynamics, and electromagnetism.

MOTION

Speed is a scalar quantity and is defined as distance divided by time. (Ex: miles per hour.)

Velocity is a vector quantity that describes speed and the direction of travel.

Magnitude of Acceleration is defined as the change in velocity divided by the time interval.

A **scalar quantity** is described only by its magnitude, whereas a **vector quantity** is described by magnitude and direction.

Acceleration is change in velocity divided by time; an object accelerates not only when it speeds up, but also when slowing down or turning. The **acceleration due to gravity** of a falling object near the Earth is a constant $9.8m/s^2$; therefore an object's magnitude increases as it falls and decreases as it rises.

Newton's Three Laws of Motion

1. An object at rest will remain at rest unless acted on by an unbalanced force. An object in motion continues in motion with the same speed and in the same direction unless acted upon by an unbalanced force. This law is often called "**The Law of Inertia**."

2. Acceleration is produced when a force acts on a mass. The greater the mass (of the object being accelerated) the greater the amount of force needed (to accelerate the object). Think of it like this: it takes a greater amount of force to push a boulder, than it does to push a feather.

3. Every action requires an equal and opposite reaction. This means that for every force, there is a reacting force both equal in size and opposite in direction. (I.e. whenever an object pushes another object, it gets pushed back in the opposite direction with equal force.)

An object's **density** is its mass divided by its volume. **Frictional forces** arise when one object tries move over or around another; the frictional forces act in the opposite direction to oppose such a motion. **Pressure** is the force per unit area which acts upon a surface.

There are **Three Important Conservation Laws** which are embodied within Newton's Laws. They offer a different and sometimes more powerful way to consider motion:

1. **Conservation of Momentum** – Embodied in Newton's first law (Law of Inertia), this reiterates that the momentum of a system is constant if no external forces act upon the system.

2. **Conservation of Energy** - Energy is neither created nor destroyed; it can be converted from one form to another (i.e. potential energy converted to kinetic energy), but the total amount of energy within the domain remains fixed.

3. **Conservation of Angular Momentum** – If the system is subjected to no external force, then the total angular momentum of a system has constant magnitude and direction. This is the common physics behind figure-skating and planetary orbits.

Energy and Forces

The energy stored within an object is called its **potential energy** – it has the potential to do work. But where does that energy come from? When gravity pulls down on an object (**gravitational energy**) the object receives potential energy. **Kinetic energy**, the energy of motion, is the energy possessed because of an object's motion.

The sum of an object's kinetic and potential energies is called the total **mechanical energy** (or, **internal energy**).

Frictional forces convert kinetic energy and gravitational potential energy into **thermal energy**. **Power** is the energy converted from one form to another, divided by the time needed to make the conversion. A **simple machine** is a device that alters the magnitude or direction of an applied force. Example: an inclined plane or lever.

Objects that move in a curved path have acceleration towards the center of that path. That acceleration is called a **centripetal acceleration. Centripetal force** is the inward force causing that object to move in the curved path. If the centripetal force is the action, the (opposite) reaction is an outwardly-directed **centrifugal force**.

THERMAL PHYSICS

Temperature and Heat

Heat and temperature are two different things. **Heat** is a measure of the work required to change the speeds in a collection of atoms or molecules. **Temperature** is a measure of the average kinetic energy of the atoms or molecules of a substance.

A **calorie** is the amount of heat required to raise the temperature of 1 gram of water by 1 degree Celsius. The **specific heat** of a substance is the ratio of the amount of heat added to a substance, divided by the mass and the temperature change of the substance.

The change of a substance from solid to liquid, or liquid to gas, etc., is called a **phase change**.

Heat of Fusion: The amount of heat required to change a unit mass of a substance from solid to liquid at the *melting point.*

Heat of Vaporization: The amount of heat needed to change a unit mass of a substance from liquid to vapor at the *boiling point.*

HEAT TRANSFER

Temperature Scales

There are three common temperature scales: **Celsius**, **Fahrenheit**, and **Kelvin**. Because it is based upon what we believe to be **absolute zero** (the lowest theoretical temperature possible before life ceases), the Kelvin scale is also known as the **absolute scale**.

Temperature Scale	Point at Which Water Freezes
Celsius	0° C
Fahrenheit	32° F
Kelvin	273K

The Two Mechanisms of Heat Transfer

Conduction: Heat transfer via conduction can occur in a substance of any phase (solid, liquid, or gas), but is mostly seen in solids.

Convection: Convection heat transfer occurs only in fluids (liquids and gases).

Both types of heat transfer are caused by molecular movement in the substance of interest.

WAVE MOTION (SOUND) AND MAGNETISM

Waves

Waves can be placed in one of two categories: **longitudinal** or **transverse**.

In a **transverse wave**, the motion of the medium is perpendicular to the motion of the wave; for example, waves on water. In a **longitudinal wave**, the motion of the medium is parallel to the motion of the wave. Sound waves are transverse waves.

A wave's **wavelength** is the distance between successive high points (**crests**) and low points (**troughs**). The **speed of a wave** is the rate at which it moves. **Frequency** – measured in **Hertz** (Hz) – is the number of repetitions, or cycles, occurring per second. The **amplitude** is the intensity (or strength) of the wave.

Sound

When vibrations disturb the air, they create sound waves. The **speed of a sound wave** is approximately 331m/s at 0° C. Human ears are capable of hearing frequencies between 20 to 16,000 Hz. The **decibel** (dB) scale is used to measure the loudness (amount of energy) of a sound wave. The scale starts at zero, which is the softest audio, and increases tenfold in intensity for every 10dB.

Magnetism is a force which either pulls magnetic materials together or pushes them apart. Iron and nickel are the most common magnetic materials. All magnetic materials are made up of tiny groups of atoms called domains. Each domain is like a mini-magnet with north and south poles. When material is magnetized, millions of domains line up.

Around every magnet there is a region in which its effects are felt, called its **magnetic field**. The magnetic field around a planet or a star is called the **magnetosphere**. Most of the planets in the Solar System, including Earth, have a magnetic field. Planets have magnetic fields because of the liquid iron in their cores. As the planets rotate, so does the iron swirl, generating electric currents which create a magnetic field. The strength of a magnet is measured in **teslas**. The Earth's magnetic field is 0.00005 teslas.

An electric current creates its own magnetic field. **Electromagnetism** (the force created together by magnetism and electricity) is one of the four fundamental forces in the Universe; the other three are gravity and the two basic forces of the atomic nucleus.

A magnet has two poles: a north pole and a south pole. Like (similar) poles (e.g. two north poles) repel each other; unlike poles attract each other. The Earth has a magnetic field that is created by electric currents within its iron core. The magnetic north pole is close to the geographic North Pole. If left to swivel freely, a magnet will turn so that its north pole points to the Earth's magnetic north pole.

Test Your Knowledge: Physics

1. A car travels at 40 miles/hr at 60° north of west. The component of the velocity in the west direction is

a) 2 miles/hr
b) 20 miles/hr
c) 40 miles/hr
d) 80 miles/hr

2. Two dogs are running towards each other. Dog #1 has a speed of 0.75 m/s and the dog #2 has a speed of 0.55 m/s. If we define the positive x direction to be the direction in which dog #1 runs, what is the velocity of dog #1 with respect to dog #2?

a) 0.75 m/s
b) 0.2 m/s
c) -1.3 m/s
d) 1.3 m/s

3. Which of the following statements concerning projectile motion is *not* true? Note that any effects due to air resistance are neglected.

a) The horizontal velocity of an object launched upwards at an angle to the horizontal is constant.
b) The acceleration is positive while the object moves upwards and negative while the object moves downward.
c) The acceleration of the object is always negative.
d) The vertical component of the velocity of an object launched upwards at an angle to the horizontal is zero at the highest point of the object's motion.

4. An object is pulled across a rough surface by a force of 20 N. If the object moves with a constant velocity and the surface has a coefficient of kinetic friction $\boldsymbol{\mu_k = 0.2}$, what is the magnitude of the normal force acting on the object?

a) 100 N
b) 10 N
c) 1 N
d) 20 N

2. A moving object has

a) Velocity.
b) Momentum.
c) Energy.
d) All of these.

3. Heat transferred between a pot of boiling water and the air above it is an example of:

a) Conduction.
b) Convection.
c) Heat of vaporization.
d) Phase change.

4. ______________ increases, decreases, or changes the direction of a force.
   a) A simple machine.
   b) Energy.
   c) Momentum.
   d) Inertia.

5. _______is a measure of the average kinetic energy of the atoms or molecules of a substance.
   a) Specific Heat
   b) Temperature
   c) Heat
   d) Force

6. Average speed is:
   a) A measure of how fast something is moving.
   b) The distance covered per unit of time.
   c) Always measured in terms of a unit of distance divided by a unit of time.
   d) All of the above.

7. Which of the following controls can change a car's velocity?
   a) The steering wheel.
   b) The brake pedal.
   c) Both A and B.
   d) None of the above.

8. The distance between two corresponding parts of a wave.
   a) Wavelength.
   b) Crest.
   c) Energy.
   d) Equidistance.

9. Unit of measurement for wave frequency.
   a) Crest.
   b) Decibel.
   c) Hertz (Hz).
   d) Period.

10. The magnetic field around a planet or a star is called a(an):
    a) Electromagnetic field.
    b) Magnetosphere.
    c) Magnetic field.
    d) Magnetic energy field.

11. The number of waves that pass a given point in one second.
    a) Trough.
    b) Energy.
    c) Crest.
    d) Frequency.

12. Unit of measurement for wave frequency.

a) Crest.
b) Decibel.
c) Hertz (Hz).
d) Period.

Test Your Knowledge: Physics – Answers

1. **c)**
2. **c)**
3. **a)**
4. **d)**
5. **d)**
6. **b)**
7. **a)**
8. **b)**
9. **c)**
10. **b)**
11. **d)**

Final Thoughts

In the end, we know that you will be successful in taking the HOAE. Although the road ahead may at times be challenging, if you continue your hard work and dedication (just like you are doing to prepare right now!), you will find that your efforts will pay off.

If you are struggling after reading this book and following our guidelines, we sincerely hope that you will take note of our advice and seek additional help. Start by asking friends about the resources that they are using. If you are still not reaching the score you want, consider getting the help of a HOAE tutor.

If you are on a budget and cannot afford a private tutoring service, there are plenty of independent tutors, including college students who are proficient in HOAE subjects. You don't have to spend thousands of dollars to afford a good tutor or review course.

We wish you the best of luck and happy studying. Most importantly, we hope you enjoy your coming years – after all, you put a lot of work into getting there in the first place.

Sincerely,
The Trivium Team

CPSIA information can be obtained
at www.ICGtesting.com
Printed in the USA
LVOW03s0351010916
502767LV00024B/238/P

9 780615 833057